HERBS, FRUITS
& VEGETABLES
for
TENNESSEE

HERBS, FRUITS
& VEGETABLES
for
TENNESSEE

James A. Fizzell
Walter Reeves
Felder Rushing

COOL
SPRINGS
PRESS

Nashville, Tennessee
A Division of Thomas Nelson, Inc.
www.ThomasNelson.com

Published by Cool Springs Press, a Division of Thomas Nelson, Inc.
P.O. Box 141000, Nashville, Tennessee, 37214.

First printing 2004
Printed in the United States of America
10 9 8 7 6 5 4 3 2 1

Managing Editor: Mary Morgan
Horticulture Editor: Michael Wenzel, Atlanta Botanical Garden
Copyeditor: Michelle Adkerson
Designer: Bill Kersey, Kersey Graphics
Production Artist: S.E. Anderson

On the cover: 'Big Boy' Tomato, photographed by Thomas Eltzroth

Photography Credits:
    Liz Ball: Rosemary, page 7; Dill, page 18; Rosemary, page 32; and
      Raspberry, page 112
    Lorenzo Gunn: Pear, page 108; and Plum, page 110
    Thomas Eltzroth: all other photographs

Visit the Thomas Nelson website at www.ThomasNelson.com

Table *of* Contents

50 Great Herbs, Vegetables, & Fruits
for Tennessee 7–115

50 Great Herbs, Vegetables, and Fruits *for* Tennessee

The keys to success in growing edibles—herbs, vegetables, and fruits—are simple: Know your plants and their needs, and know your site and how to make it meet those needs. Edible plants are most productive during the growing season—the dates between the last frost in spring and the first frost in fall. This is definitely the case with annuals, which do not survive our cold winters. Check with your Extension Agent for the average dates of last and first frosts in your area, since they will determine your planting time and your harvest season.

Soils and Fertilizers

Plants need adequate nutrients to grow properly. They receive nutrients from the soil, from rain, and from the fertilizer you add. Have your soil tested to see what nutrients are missing that your plants need. The best place to have this done is through the University of Tennessee Extension Service. Your County Extension office–listed in the phone book under "County Government"—can tell you how to package and submit a soil sample.

Once your soil has been analyzed, you'll receive a report telling you the pH of your soil (how acidic or alkaline it is) and how much and what type of fertilizer to use. pH is important because it helps determine whether your plants can absorb the nutrients in the soil. The fertilizer recommendation will focus primarily on the big three nutrients—nitrogen, phosphorus, and potassium (N, P, K). Nitrogen promotes the growth of roots, stems, and leaves. Phosphorus helps plants store energy. And potassium is important to help the plants manufacture sugar and starch. All three are needed, but in the right amounts.

The fertilizer recommendation you receive will probably say add x pounds per 100 square feet of 10-10-10, or 16-4-8, or some other formula. Those

Rosemary

7

numbers are expressing percentages—16-4-8 means a fertilizer that's 16 percent nitrogen, 4 percent phosphorus, and 8 percent potassium. So the recommended ratio is 4:1:2 (dividing all the percentages by the smallest— 4). Knowing this lets you adapt the recommendation to another fertilizer strength—20-5-10, for example—or to organic fertilizers if you prefer.

Time spent preparing your planting area correctly pays huge dividends down the road. Clear away any turf and weeds, including roots, and dig the soil to a depth of 10 inches, breaking up big clods and removing rocks and roots as you work. Add a layer of organic matter—composted pine bark, composted animal manure, or homemade compost—sufficient to make the bed about $2/3$ soil and $1/3$ organic matter. Mix it together well, then put in your fertilizer, lime, or other recommended additives, and mix again.

Herbs

Herbs are easy to grow—easier, in fact, than familiar vegetables and fruits. Many thrive in infertile soil with minimal care, since with too many nutrients and too much water, they may grow bigger but be less flavorful. And the flavorful leaves are what most herbs are all about. Herbs can be grown in beds to themselves, mixed in with flowers, or put at the edge of the vegetable garden. Many can even be grown as potted plants and brought indoors to overwinter and provide a fresh harvest year-round. Most herbs need full sun, and insects and diseases usually don't bother them much. Be especially careful about spraying insecticides or other

Potatoes

8

Raspberries

controls on or near herbs—their leaves are very absorbent and filled with oils, and it's the leaves you'll likely be eating.

Vegetables

It's best to locate your vegetable garden where it's accessible but doesn't intrude on your living spaces. Vegetable gardens can be lovely—and edible landscaping is all the rage—but even so, they tend to be messy, and good culture doesn't necessarily go along with good looks. Site your garden where it receives at least eight to ten hours of sun every day. To avoid roots of shrubs and trees infiltrating the garden, put it at least as far away as the height of the trees or shrubs. Make the garden only as large as you can tend comfortably. And site it within easy reach of the hose—vegetables need at least an inch of water each week, and if nature doesn't provide it, you must.

Fruits

Your choice of fruits depends on your space and your time. Strawberries can be put in your vegetable garden; they require little more maintenance than the vegetables. Bush berries—blueberries, blackberries, raspberries—require more space, more pruning, and more spraying. And tree fruits—apples, peaches, plums—require a good bit of room, even for dwarf trees, plus a real time commitment to do all the pruning, watering, fertilizing, and controlling pests that will be necessary to make the trees attractive and productive. Like vegetables, fruits need full sun and an inch of water each week.

HERBS

Contents

Basil

Ocimum basilicum

The Queen of the Kitchen

A familiar and popular herb, basil is the basis for pesto. Many cooks consider basil the premier culinary herb. Every gardener needs at least one basil plant for fresh leaves to toss into casseroles, sauces, and salads or to add to eggs, fish, pizza, spaghetti, and tacos. Fresh basil sliced into strips, sprinkled over sliced tomatoes, then topped with a little excellent quality olive oil just can't be beat.

Top Reasons to Plant

○ Fragrant, tasty leaves
○ Excellent with tomato-based dishes
○ Tolerates light shade
○ Grows indoors over winter
○ Lots of varieties available

Useful Hint

For winter use, trim plants back, pot up one or two of them, then place the plants indoors in a bright, humid place such as over the kitchen sink.

Height/Width
6 to 18 inches x 8 to 14 inches

Planting Location
- Well-drained soil
- Full sun to light shade

Planting
- Sow seeds indoors about two months before frost-free date.
- *Or* buy plants at your local garden center or nursery.
- Plant outdoors when night temperatures are 50 degrees Fahrenheit or higher.
- Space plants 12 inches apart.
- *Or* direct-seed into the garden in hills 12 inches apart, thinning plants to one plant per hill when seedlings become large enough to handle.
- Water well and mulch lightly.

Watering
- Basil plants cannot withstand wilting.
- Water as needed to ensure an inch of water each week.

Fertilizing
- No fertilizer is needed if plants are growing well.

Suggestions for Vigorous Growth
- When plants are 6 inches tall and growing vigorously, pinch out growing tips to stimulate branching and to keep plants from flowering.
- If flowers form, pinch them off, and let the plants regrow.

Easy Tip
In additional to sweet basil, try one of the many other cultivars and forms for hints of lemon, cinnamon, or licorice.

Harvesting
- Harvest sprigs as needed but before flowers form.
- Cut each stem with a sharp knife or scissors, leaving two leaves on each stem to develop into new shoots.
- Complete harvest before first frost.

Pest Control
- Aphids and mites can attack basil— pinch off affected shoots or spray with insecticidal soap.
- Carefully wash off insecticidal soap before eating.

Recommended Selections
- Sweet basil is the best known and most easily available form.
- Lemon basil (*Ocimum basilicum* 'Citriodorum') has a fresh lemon flavor.
- 'Napolitano' has large crinkled leaves.
- 'Cinnamon' has a cinnamon flavor and fragrance.
- 'Dark Opal' and 'Purple Ruffles' have strong flavors and are better for ornamental use than for eating.
- 'Siam Queen' has a licorice flavor.
- 'Minimum' has small leaves and a compact form.
- 'Russian Blue' is a large plant with purple stems that attracts bees and hummingbirds.

Chives
Allium schoenoprasum

A Delicate-Tasting Member of the Onion Family

Chives are perennial plants (plants that go dormant outdoors in winter and return the next spring) belonging to the onion family. They produce foot-tall clumps of hollow, upright leaves. If allowed to go to flower, they make mounds of pretty, lavender-pink flowers that are also edible and have a taste similar to the leaves. Chives add a delicate onionlike flavor to soups, stews, salads, omelets, sauces, and of course, baked potatoes with sour cream.

Top Reasons to Plant

○ Delicate onion flavor
○ Pretty, edible flowers
○ Good in a variety of settings
○ Grows well in containers
○ Nice in an herb garden, perennial garden, and vegetable garden, or as edging along a mixed border
○ Easy to grow

Useful Hint

Another member of the onion family is the perennial garlic chives (*Allium tuberosum*), which produce long, flat leaves with a garlic flavor. They take the heat better than true chives and don't die back in fall.

Height/Width
12 inches x 24 inches

Planting Location
- Well-drained soil
- Sun or light shade
- Corner of the garden where they won't be disturbed—they're perennial and the size of the clumps increases each year

Planting
- Set out plants in early spring.
- Space plants 12 inches apart.
- Water well.
- *Or* in early spring sow seeds on the soil surface and cover lightly.
- Thin to 12 inches apart when seedlings are up and growing vigorously.
- Seed-grown plants are more variable than divisions, so dig out any with smaller leaves.

Watering
- Water well during dry weather.

Fertilizing
- No fertilizer is needed.

Suggestions for Vigorous Growth
- Keep plants clipped to eliminate flowering.
- Flowers make the leaves tough and unusable, and also reseed.

Easy Tip

Chives of all types have a tendency to spread—planting them in containers keeps them under control.

- Divide plants every three years, separating into bunches of five or six bulblets each, and replant or give away.

Harvesting
- Harvest leaves by snipping them off with sharp scissors.
- Dig up the plant before frost, shake dirt off the roots, replant in pot using potting soil, and move the plant indoors to a sunny spot; you'll have chives all winter.

Pest Control
- Thrips may appear—use insecticidal soap for control, and wash leaves well before eating.

Recommended Selections
- Both garlic chives and common chives are good and distinctive— try them both.

Cilantro-Coriander

Coriandrum sativum

An Herb with Two Uses— Leaves and Seeds

Cilantro and coriander are two stages of the same annual plant. The parsleylike foliage, which is picked before the seeds form, is called cilantro. In the U.S., the number one use of cilantro is in salsa. Mature seeds, which are collected and dried for use in cooking and baking, are called coriander. Coriander is a major ingredient in curry powder, widely used in East Indian cooking.

Top Reasons to Plant

○ Dual uses—leaves and seeds
○ Leaves excellent in salsa and other Mexican dishes, as well as Asian cuisine
○ Seeds useful in East Indian foods
○ Easy to grow

Useful Hint

Summer sowings may bolt (send up flower stalks) before the rosettes of leaves form—leave these flower stalks to mature into coriander seeds.

Height/Width
24 inches x 18 inches

Planting Location
• Well-drained, well-tilled soil
• Sun

Planting
• Sow seed in the garden in very early spring, with repeated sowings every three weeks for a season-long supply.
• Place seeds an inch apart in rows 2 feet apart.
• Do not thin plants.
• Keep seedbed moist until seedlings sprout.

Watering
• Provide an inch of water each week if nature doesn't.

Fertilizing
• No fertilizer is needed.

Suggestions for Vigorous Growth
• Hoe or pull any weeds that appear.

Harvesting
• In hot weather, plants quickly flower and set seed.
• Harvest fully developed rosettes of cilantro leaves as soon as there are signs of flower stalks.

Easy Tip
Seeding directly into the garden is preferable to buying transplants—the transplants bolt (send up flower stalks) too quickly.

• For coriander, allow seedheads to turn tan before harvesting.
• Tie a paper bag over the flower clusters to catch the seeds as they mature and drop.
• Clean out and dispose of any immature seed and foliage before using the seeds.

Pest Control
• Mites may appear—control with insecticidal soap, and wash leaves carefully before eating.

Recommended Selections
• 'Santo' is a slow-bolting cilantro if you're not interested in coriander seeds.

Dill

Anethum graveolens

A Common Herb with Bountiful Culinary Talents

Dill deserves a place in every garden because of its many culinary uses. Just a few plants provide enough dill for most households. The soft, fernlike foliage, called dill weed, is used fresh. Small plants harvested in spring and fall are known as salad dill. Both are great in soups, salads, egg, fish, and poultry dishes. The flower heads and dried seeds are important for pickling processes.

Top Reasons to Plant

○ Feathery leaves that accent many dishes
○ Seeds useful for pickling and breads
○ Easy to grow
○ Self-seeds readily
○ Attracts swallowtail butterflies
○ Tolerates some shade

Useful Hint

Dill reseeds readily—dig up new seedlings and transplant them where you want them in the garden.

18

Height/Width
48 inches x 18 inches

Planting Location
- Well-prepared moist soil
- Sun or partial shade (filtered sun all day or shade part of the day)

Planting
- Sow seeds or set out plants in early spring.
- Place seeds an inch apart in rows 1 foot apart.
- Thin seedlings when 6 inches tall—use seedlings as salad dill.
- If using started plants, set them 1 foot apart in beds or 2 feet apart in rows.
- Sow seeds throughout summer to ensure constant supply.
- Keep watered until established or until seeds sprout and are growing vigorously.

Watering
- Water deeply in weeks without an inch of rain.

Fertilizing
- No fertilizer is required.

Suggestions for Vigorous Growth
- These plants need little care once they begin growing.
- Keeping foliage cut back delays flowering and seed-setting.
- Late in the season, allow a few heads to mature and drop seed to produce seedlings for the next year.

Easy Tip
If black swallowtail butterfly larvae—large black-and-yellow-striped caterpillars—visit your dill, collect the chrysalises that form; then hatch them in a screen cage for a fun summertime project with kids.

Harvesting
- Harvest salad dill at 6 to 10 inches tall.
- Cut flower heads in full bloom—use either fresh or dried.
- To save seeds, cut heads when seeds are mature but before the heads begin to shatter.
- Hang the heads upside down indoors in paper bags to catch seeds.
- Dry dill leaves and flowers, and then store in airtight containers to use later.

Pest Control
- No serious pests trouble these plants, which are beloved by black swallowtail butterfly larvae—but they don't each much.

Recommended Selections
- 'Florist's Dill' is a Dutch strain widely used in the international cut-flower trade—its feathery foliage and flat clusters of flowers make great filler in arrangements.
- 'Dukat' produces much more foliage before forming seeds than most dills.

Fennel

Foeniculum vulgare, Foeniculum vulgare var. *dulce*

Herb or Vegetable? It's Both!

Fennel (*F. vulgare*) is a European herb known for its aromatic seeds and tender, fragrant leaves. It has a wonderful flavor similar to anise or licorice. Florence fennel (*F. vulgare* var. *dulce*), often called finocchio, develops a bulblike base used raw or steamed. Both types of fennel are tender perennials grown as annuals. If you like fennel—or swallowtail butterflies—you may want six or more plants.

Top Reasons to Plant

○ Feathery leaves taste good with fish, pork, and veal, and in soups and sauces
○ Bulb excellent grilled or roasted
○ Attracts butterflies
○ Self-seeds readily

Useful Hint

The plants that produce bulbs and those that produce leaves and seeds are very different plants—if you want the bulbs, you must plant Florence fennel.

Height/Width
4 feet x 3 feet

Planting Location
- Well-prepared soil
- Far enough from other plants to give fennel room to grow
- Sun

Planting
- Start seeds indoors six weeks before the last frost, or sow them directly into the garden after the last heavy freeze.
- Its taproot sometimes makes this plant difficult to transplant.
- Thin seedlings to 8 inches apart when they are 4 inches tall.
- If started indoors, plant the seeds in peat pots, which can be buried so the roots aren't disturbed.
- Keep the seedbed moist until the seedlings are visible and growing vigorously.

Watering
- Water deeply in weeks without an inch of rain.

Fertilizing
- No fertilizer is needed.

Suggestions for Vigorous Growth
- Keep foliage cut back to delay flowers and seeds.
- Cover fennel bulbs with soil when they are 2 to 3 inches in diameter.
- Late in the season, let a few plants set seed and let the seed drop to produce plants for next year.

Easy Tip
Florence fennel develops a bulblike rosette of foliage and must be harvested before the plant sends up a flower stalk.

Harvesting
- Harvest tender leaves when plants are 6 to 10 inches tall.
- To harvest seeds, cut the heads when the seeds mature but before the heads shatter.
- Hang the heads upside down in brown paper bags indoors to finish drying.
- Tie harvested leaves into small bundles and hang them in a warm dry place to dry.
- Store dried leaves and seeds in airtight containers.
- Harvest bulbs before the plant flowers.
- In cool fall weather, the harvest may extend through light frosts.

Pest Control
- No serious pests bother this plant, which is beloved by swallowtail butterflies—the caterpillars don't eat much.

Recommended Selections
- Bronze fennel ('Purpurascens'), a form of common fennel, has the same edible leaves and seeds, and its beautiful bronze-red foliage is highly ornamental.

French Tarragon

Artemisia dracunculus

*A Wonderful Culinary Herb
That Belongs in Every Garden*

French tarragon is a 2-foot-tall
perennial herb of outstanding
character. It is the most important
herb in French cuisine, used in
béarnaise, tartar, rémoulade,
and hollandaise sauces; in salad
dressings, mayonnaise, and soups;
and in egg, pork, or chicken dishes.
It also makes an outstanding
vinegar. Thomas Jefferson, who
loved all things French, is believed
to have been an early promoter
of tarragon in America.

Top Reasons to Plant

○ Distinctive flavor highly valued
  in the kitchen
○ Perennial
○ Easy to grow
○ Few pests and diseases
○ Tolerates light shade
○ Good in containers

Useful Hint

Mexican tarragon (*Tagetes lucida*) grows
much better than French tarragon in
the hottest parts of the South—it has a
similar, but less refined, flavor and can
be substituted in cooking in place of
"real" tarragon.

Height/Width
2 feet x 2 feet

Planting Location
• Well-drained, fertile soil
• Sun or light shade

Planting
• Set out plants in early spring.
• Space plants 1 foot apart.
• Water well.

Watering
• Water deeply in weeks without an inch of rain.

Fertilizing
• No fertilizer is needed.

Suggestions for Vigorous Growth
• Pinch newly started plants to encourage branching.
• Harvest leaves often to encourage a new crop of leaves.
• Divide plants every three or four years.

Easy Tip
Plant tarragon in a part of the garden where it won't be disturbed by other gardening activities—it's a perennial and will come back year after year.

Harvesting
• Begin harvesting leaves as soon as the plants are growing vigorously.
• Be aware that tarragon loses most of its flavor when dried.
• Lift a few plants in the fall, clip them back to a convenient size, pot them, and move them indoors to a cool, bright place for fresh tarragon all winter.

Pest Control
• No serious pests bother this plant.

Recommended Selections
• Be sure to buy vegetatively propagated—not seed-grown—plants; tarragon does not come true from seed, and seeded types are vastly inferior.

Greek Oregano

Origanum heracleoticum

A Favorite Herb for Italian Dishes

An easily grown, semihardy perennial, oregano—like mint—is sometimes a bit too easily grown. Common oregano (*Origanum vulgare*) spreads rapidly and widely, so restrict it by creating barriers or planting it in a lined, raised bed. Better still, plant Greek oregano (*Origanum heracleoticum*), which is tastier and less aggressive.

Top Reasons to Plant

○ Excellent in pizzas, pasta sauces, and other Italian dishes
○ Easy to grow, spreading rapidly
○ Does well in containers

Useful Hint

In colder parts of the state, put 6 to 8 inches of pine straw over the plants to provide some winter protection—remove it in the spring before growth begins.

Height/Width
1 to 2 feet x 1^1/$_2$ feet

Planting Location
- Well-drained, average soil
- Sun

Planting
- Purchase vegetatively propagated plants from a reliable source—seed-grown plants may be flavorless.
- Common oregano (*Origanum vulgare*), sold in many garden centers, grows into an invasive plant with little, if any, flavor.
- Before buying the plant, taste a leaf to be sure it has good, strong flavor.
- Set out plants in very early spring—oregano can stand a freeze.
- Space plants 18 inches apart in 18-inch rows.

Watering
- Water deeply if less than an inch of rain has fallen during the week.

Fertilizing
- No fertilizer is needed.

Easy Tip
Virtually all oregano seed is common oregano, so this is one plant you'll need to buy—from a reputable source.

Suggestions for Vigorous Growth
- Divide plants in spring or fall.
- This plant needs little care.
- Harvest often to encourage new, tender, flavorful leaves.

Harvesting
- Cut stalks as soon as flowers appear, usually May.
- If plant sets seed, now leaf production stops.
- Dry oregano quickly, placing branches on a window screen, then strip the leaves and store in them in airtight containers.

Pest Control
- No serious pests bother this plant.

Recommended Selections
- Make sure you're buying real Greek oregano.

Lavender

Lavandula species

A Wonderful Fragrant Herb with Uses in the Kitchen

While cooking isn't the first use that comes to mind for lavender, the flowers and buds have some excellent culinary uses. They can be added to vinegars or jams. Mix them into sugar cookie dough for an elegant, unusual cookie. Crystallize the flowers to decorate desserts, especially chocolate ones. And they add a unique flavor to custards and salads.

Top Reasons to Plant

- Lovely, fragrant flowers
- Decorative appearance
- Tolerates dry soils
- Long-lived perennial
- Excellent edging for decorative herb gardens

Useful Hint

Plant lavender in a raised bed or mound with plenty of room between plants for the air to circulate—this helps reduce problems from high humidity.

Height/Width
1 to 3 feet x 1 to 3 feet

Planting Location
- Well-drained, sandy soil
- Sun

Planting
- Add lots of organic matter or sand to clay soils to ensure excellent drainage.
- Set plants 1 to 3 feet apart depending on their ultimate spread.
- Water well with a transplant solution.

Watering
- Once established, this plant tolerates drought.
- But, lavender blooms and grows better with regular watering—an inch each week if the soil is dry.

Fertilizing
- No fertilizer is needed—too much reduces the scent and flavor.

Suggestions for Vigorous Growth
- Cut back in early spring by about half and by one-third in early fall if you don't want the plant to become woody.

Easy Tip

Be careful which lavender you choose—the best-known one, English lavender (*Lavandula angustifolia*), has a hard time with our heat and humidity. Look for hybrids such as 'Dutch', 'Provence', and 'Grosso'.

Harvesting
- Harvest flower spikes when flowers fully open and are bright in color.
- Cut flowers on a dry day.
- Dry in small groups tied together and hung upside down in a dark, dry place.
- Once dried, stems can be used immediately or stored as is in an airtight container, or buds can be stripped for potpourri or culinary use.

Pest Control
- Fungal diseases or rot may be a problem if plants are overcrowded or receive too much water.

Recommended Selections
- 'Grosso' is best for making lavender wands and for dried arrangements since the flowers stay on the stem well.
- If you are using just the buds, try 'Provence'; its buds release easily from the stem.

Mint

Mentha species

An Aggressive Spreader Needing Careful Handling

Mints are easily grown perennial ground covers valued as flavorings in teas, ice cream, candies, and gum. Each of the many varieties has a distinctive flavor. The most commonly grown are peppermint (*Mentha* x *piperita*) and spearmint (*Mentha spicata*). All types spread rapidly, so help contain them by using concrete blocks or timbers buried with their tops just above ground to create a barrier.

Top Reasons to Plant

- Tasty, tangy leaves with many uses
- Many varieties with distinctive flavors
- Tolerates some shade
- Willing grower

Useful Hint

Make sure you're buying the plant you want by checking the label, then pinching a leaf and checking the fragrance.

Height/Width
1 to 2 feet x 3 feet or more

Planting Location
- Site where their spreading can be contained
- Lined, raised beds work well
- Well-drained, moist soil
- Sun to partial shade

Planting
- Set out started plants anytime during the growing season.
- Separate different types with barriers— or they will intermingle.
- Space plants 2 feet apart.
- Keep plants well watered until they are growing vigorously.

Watering
- Provide an inch of water a week if nature doesn't.

Fertilizing
- No fertilizer is needed.

Suggestions for Vigorous Growth
- Keep well weeded.
- Renew growth by plowing beds in fall to a depth of 6 inches in order to cut up underground stems and stimulate spring growth.
- Mulch in winter with 3 to 4 inches of pine straw to protect plants in the coldest parts of the state—remove mulch before growth begins in spring.

Easy Tip

Crush a leaf from a few specimens of the type of mint you want, then buy the ones with the strongest aroma.

Harvesting
- Cut sprigs of mint anytime.
- When flower buds begin appearing, harvest sprigs 6 to 10 inches long as needed.
- Dry small bunches of sprigs by hanging them upside down in a warm, dry place.
- Strip the leaves after the bunches dry, and store them in airtight containers.

Pest Control
- Verticillium wilt is the most damaging disease—don't plant mint where you have grown tomatoes or potatoes; they also carry the disease and may infect the soil.

Recommended Selections
- Apple mint (*Mentha suaveolens*) has a fruity flavor and aroma.
- Pineapple mint (*Mentha suaveolens* 'Variegata') has green and white variegated leaves with a pineapple flavor.
- Corsican mint (*Mentha requienii*) carries a crème-de-menthe fragrance.

Parsley

Petroselinum crispum

A Pretty Herb Good for More Than Garnish

Virtually everyone recognizes parsley, a frequent garnish on plates served in restaurants. Parsley leaves are also used in various dishes, soups, and sauces. For cooking, Italian parsley, which has flat, shiny leaves, is much better than curly parsley, as it has a much stronger flavor. Parsley is actually a biennial (growing leaves only the first year, then flowering and dying the next), but most gardeners grow it as an annual.

Top Reasons to Plant

- Pretty garnish
- Tasty addition to cooked dishes
- Parsley root is good in soups and stews
- Tolerates some shade
- Requires little care
- Nice decorative edging to herb or vegetable garden

Useful Hint

Dig up one or two plants before the first frost, shake off as much soil as possible, then pot in artificial potting soil; set the pot in a sunny window where you can snip the leaves all winter.

Height/Width
1 foot x 1 foot

Planting Location
- Moist, well-drained soil
- Sun or partial shade

Planting
- Sow seed outdoors—they take four or more weeks to germinate.
- Space seeds 1 inch apart in rows 1 foot apart.
- Thin seedlings to 6 or 8 inches apart.
- Sow seed indoors—at 70 degrees Fahrenheit, under lights, with pots covered by plastic wrap; seeds germinate in about a week.
- Transplant small seedlings into peat pots to plant later in the garden.
- Space transplants or purchased plants 1 foot apart.

Watering
- Provide an inch of water during weeks without that much rainfall.

Fertilizing
- No fertilizer is needed.

Easy Tip
After its first year, parsley bolts (sends up a flower stalk, then seeds) immediately the next spring—replant it every year.

Suggestions for Vigorous Growth
- For fresh leaves all season, clip off the entire top half of the plant and let the remainder regrow.
- Harvest the leaves regularly.

Harvesting
- Harvest the leaves as they mature, clipping the oldest leaves as needed.
- Protect parsley from cold with a mound of pine straw, so you can harvest leaves all winter.

Pest Control
- Mites may appear—if so, spray with insecticidal soap, but be sure to thoroughly wash the leaves before using.

Recommended Selections
- Try both the curly and flat-leaf (Italian) forms of parsley.

31

Rosemary
Rosmarinus officinalis

A Pretty Evergreen with a Piney Flavor

Rosemary is a small, woody shrub only marginally hardy in the coldest parts of the state. Even there, gardeners grow it as a perennial, dutifully lifting and potting the plant for overwintering indoors. The needlelike leaves add a distinctive, vaguely "piney" flavor to a variety of dishes. Leaves are used in soups, stews, and sauces, as well as with poultry and meat dishes. It can be trimmed to any size and shape, but it usually is kept to about a foot tall.

Top Reasons to Plant

○ Attractive evergreen shrub
○ Lends distinctive flavor to dishes
○ Leaves release a piney scent when brushed
○ Pretty blue flowers

Useful Hint

As a bonus to its tasty leaves, rosemary has beautiful blue or white flowers in early spring.

Height/Width
1 to 3 feet x 1 to 2 feet

Planting Location
- Well-drained soil
- Sun or partial shade
- Containers

Planting
- Set plants in the garden after danger of frost has passed.
- Place plants at same depth as in pots.
- Space plants 18 inches apart.
- If growing in containers, use one plant per 12-inch pot.

Watering
- Once established, rosemary tolerates all but the most severe droughts.
- When growing rosemary in pots, do not allow the soil to dry out completely.

Fertilizing
- No fertilizer is needed in the garden.
- In containers, use liquid fertilizer once in spring and again in summer.

Suggestions for Vigorous Growth
- Rosemary requires very little attention.
- Poorly drained soil may cause root or stem rot—correcting the drainage cures the problem.

Easy Tip
Rosemary plants make attractive potted shrubs when trimmed to shape and can be used to create interesting topiaries, as well.

Harvesting
- Cut sprigs 8 to 10 inches long, and strip leaves as needed.
- Tie sprigs in loose bunches and hang upside down to dry indoors in a warm, dark spot.
- Strip leaves from dried stems, and store them in an airtight container.

Pest Control
- No serious pests or diseases bother this plant.

Recommended Selections
- 'Athens Blue Spires', 'Arp', and 'Hill's Hardy' withstand cold weather well.
- 'Prostrata' is a creeping type excellent for edging.

Sage
Salvia officinalis

A Fragrant Herb with a Clean Flavor

Many centuries ago, sage was believed to increase mental capacity. It probably doesn't do that, but it certainly does add a distinctive, clean flavor to poultry stuffing, sausages, vinegars, egg dishes, soups, and herbal butters. Sage is a hardy, semiwoody perennial plant that makes a loose shrub about 2 feet tall. Its delicate blue flowers are quite attractive.

Top Reasons to Plant

○ Excellent fresh or dried in a variety of dishes
○ Easy to grow
○ Pretty blue, pink, or white flowers
○ Low maintenance

Useful Hint

Do not prune sage severely just before the onset of winter, or its survival may be adversely affected.

Height/Width
12 to 30 inches x 24 inches

Planting Location
• Well-drained soil
• Sun

Planting
• Set out plants in spring as soon as the ground can be worked.
• Space plants 15 to 18 inches apart where they won't shade other plants.

Watering
• Sage tolerates dry soil but appreciates an inch of water in weeks when there isn't that much rain.

Fertilizing
• No fertilizer is needed.

Suggestions for Vigorous Growth
• Keep weeds under control by pulling or hoeing them.
• Prune established plants each spring to remove dead or damaged branches and to develop more compact plants.

Harvesting
• Clip sprigs 8 to 10 inches long when leaves are fully developed.

Easy Tip
Sage may be used fresh—a few leaves give a nice twang to a salad—but are usually used dried.

• Hang sprigs upside down in a warm, dark place indoors to dry.
• Strip dried leaves from stems, and store them in airtight containers.

Pest Control
• Mites may be a problem—control with insecticidal soap, making sure to wash leaves thoroughly before eating.
• In wet years, diseases may damage some stems—cut off affected stems before diseases can spread.

Recommended Selections
• 'Berggarten' has unusually large leaves and a bushy habit.
• 'Tricolor', with purple, white, and green leaves, and 'Icterina', with green, yellow, and cream leaves, are sold as ornamentals but also can be used in the kitchen.

Sweet Marjoram

Origanum majorana

A Favorite Mediterranean Herb with Many Uses

Marjoram is a tender perennial usually grown as an annual. It's similar to oregano but with a finer texture and more delicate, sweeter flavor. The leaves and flowers make tasty additions to many dishes containing meat and poultry, fish, green vegetables, carrots, eggs, mushrooms, and tomatoes. Dried, it makes a nice addition to herb wreaths, especially culinary ones. The Greeks used marjoram to make wreaths and garlands for weddings and funerals.

Top Reasons to Plant

○ Nice addition to many dishes
○ Good for dried herb projects
○ Easy to grow
○ Prefers poor soil

Useful Hint

For fresh sweet marjoram all winter, lift a plant or two from the garden in fall, pot them, and move them indoors.

Height/Width
10 to 12 inches x 8 to 10 inches

Planting Location
- Well-drained, infertile soil
- Sun
- Containers

Planting
- Set out plants in spring after danger of frost has passed.
- Space plants 8 to 10 inches apart.
- Or sow seeds in spring, and thin seedlings to 6 or 8 inches apart.

Watering
- Marjoram requires little if any water beyond rainfall.

Fertilizing
- No fertilizer is needed.

Suggestions for Vigorous Growth
- Control weeds until plants are well established.
- Trim foliage to keep plants in shape.

Easy Tip
Fresh marjoram can be frozen in ice cube trays or foil and stored for up to two weeks.

Harvesting
- Cut sprigs several inches long as soon as the first flowers appear.
- Continue clipping sprigs to stimulate more production.
- Use leaves fresh, or dry them quickly and remove the leaves before storing them in an airtight container.

Pest Control
- No serious pests trouble this plant.

Recommended Selections
- Plant the species.

Thyme
Thymus vulgaris

A Popular Kitchen Herb with Pretty Flowers

Thyme is a spreading perennial ground cover up to 12 inches tall and many times as wide (unless contained). It's popular in many types of dishes, including salads, stocks, stews, stuffings, vinegars, meat and fish, sausages, vegetables, breads, and honey. It's attractive enough for an edging in the flower garden (assuming you don't hit it with the insecticides), bearing small pink or purplish flowers that attract legions of bees.

Top Reasons to Plant

○ Tiny, tasty leaves
○ Attractive flowers
○ Spreading habit
○ Useful as edging or ground cover
○ Attracts bees

Useful Hint

Thyme was once used medicinally— eating a soup of beer and thyme was believed to overcome shyness, and Scots drank wild thyme tea for strength and courage, and to prevent nightmares.

Height/Width

1 foot x 1 to 3 feet

Planting Location

- Well-drained, not overly fertile soil
- Sun or partial shade
- Containers

Planting

- Set out plants in spring.
- Space plants 12 inches apart in all directions.
- If planting several varieties, separate with timbers, bricks, or tiles to prevent them from mingling.

Watering

- Water only if there has been no rain in several weeks.

Fertilizing

- No fertilizer is needed—overly rich soils or fertilizer encourage rampant, flavorless growth.

Suggestions for Vigorous Growth

- Trim this plant often to keep it inbounds.
- Keep it weeded.
- Replant every three or four years—old plantings become messy and woody.
- Stick cuttings in the ground—thyme roots readily.

Easy Tip

One plant is enough for fresh use, but you may want to grow several varieties because each has a different taste.

Harvesting

- Clip off 6- to 8-inch-long stems to use fresh or to dry.
- Tie stems in loose bunches to dry quickly on a window screen.
- Strip leaves from dried stems, store leaves in an airtight container.
- Lift a few plants in fall, trim to shape, pot them, and move them to a cool, bright place indoors.

Pest Control

- Outdoor plants have no serious pests.
- Mites may appear indoors—spray with insecticidal soap, and wash leaves well before eating.

Recommended Selections

- English thyme has flat, green leaves.
- French thyme has superior flavor.
- 'Orange Balsam' features a distinctive, citrus fragrance.
- Lemon thyme (*Thymus citriodorus*) is lemony—there are several cultivars.

VEGETABLES

Contents

Asparagus

Asparagus officinalis

A Spring Classic with Juicy, Tasty Spears

A cool-climate perennial plant fairly well adapted to all but the hottest areas of the South, asparagus is native to Europe and Asia, where it has been cultivated for more than two thousand years. The earliest settlers brought it to America, and abandoned plantings still can be found around old farmsteads and in volunteer patches along roadsides where it has "escaped" from cultivation.

Top Reasons to Plant

- Excellent fresh from the garden
- Returns year after year
- Few pests or diseases

Useful Hint

Asparagus plants are either male or female, with the females using their energy to form seeds while the males devote their energy to making spears—recent introductions are either mostly male or all male to increase the harvest.

Planting Location
- Well-drained, sandy soil with lots of organic matter
- Sun

Planting
- Dig a trench 6 inches deep and 15 inches wide.
- Set plants in the trench 1 foot apart with their buds pointing up.
- Spread roots in a uniform pattern around each crown (point where roots and buds meet).
- Place 2 inches of soil from the trench over the crowns.
- Water thoroughly to settle the soil.
- Gradually cover crowns with remaining soil as plants grow during their first season.

Watering
- Provide an inch of water each week during the growing season if there hasn't been that much rainfall.

Fertilizing
- After harvest each year, feed asparagus with 10-10-10 fertilizer at a rate of 1 pound per 100 square feet.

Suggestions for Vigorous Growth
- Prepare the bed well before planting—it will last many years before reworking becomes necessary.
- Keep weeds under control by hoeing, hand-pulling, and applying a deep mulch.
- In the first year, plants produce weak, spindly growth; as their root systems grow, spears become larger and more numerous each year.

Easy Tip
Plant the latest introductions—asparagus beds last a long time, so it pays to plant the very best possible.

Harvesting
- Do not harvest at all until the third season.
- In the third season, harvest for only three weeks.
- In years thereafter, harvest spears from the time they appear until late May or June.
- Cut spears when they are 6 to 8 inches long.
- Discontinue harvesting when spears become noticeably smaller.

Pest Control
- No serious pests bother this plant.

Recommended Selections
- 'Jersey Giant', a mostly male hybrid, produces a good yield.
- 'Jersey Knight', mostly male, resists diseases and produces well.
- 'Syn 4-362', a mostly male hybrid, produces large spears.
- 'Syn 53', mostly male, is a newer hybrid.
- 'UC-157', a mostly male hybrid, produces a large yield.
- 'Viking KBC', a mostly male hybrid, produces well.

Bean
Phaseolus vulgaris

Our Most Diverse Garden Vegetable

Most beans are grown for their seeds and pods. The tender pods, used before the seeds mature, are called snap beans because the pods snap when bent. Shell beans, such as limas, are harvested before maturity, and the seeds removed. Dry beans are grown for the seeds, which are allowed to mature before harvest and are then shelled from the pods for use.

Top Reasons to Plant

- Tender at the snap stage
- Produce shell beans before maturity
- Provide dry beans after maturity

Useful Hint

Bean plants may be either bush types or runners—the latter need supports on which to grow.

Planting Location
- Well-drained, fertile soil
- Sun or light shade part of the day

Planting
- Sow seeds about two weeks before the last expected frost.
- Continue planting every two or three weeks until the first of August for a summer-long crop.
- Plant seeds of bush beans 2 to 3 inches apart.
- Plant seeds of pole beans 6 inches apart in rows along a fence or trellis.
- *Or* sow seeds of pole beans in hills of 6 seeds around poles set 3 feet apart.
- Cover seeds with 1 inch of soil.
- For pole beans, make a three-pole teepee tied at the top or drive individual poles securely into the ground in each hill to support the vines.

Watering
- Provide an inch of water each week if it hasn't rained that amount.

Fertilizing
- No fertilizer is needed beyond initial fertilizing of the garden.

Suggestions for Vigorous Growth
- If beans have not been grown in the garden before, add legume inoculants to the soil before planting—these bacteria help the plants absorb nitrogen.
- If soil insects damage roots or stems before they emerge, apply a granular or water-mixed garden soil insecticide according to label directions to protect seeds as they germinate.
- Weed beans regularly.

Easy Tip
Do not work in the bean patch when beans are wet—doing so spreads leaf diseases, such as rust and bacterial blight.

Harvesting
- Pick snap beans when pods are firm and fully elongated but before seeds begin to swell.
- Pick beans regularly to keep plants producing.
- Pick shell beans when seeds are tender, green, and fully developed.
- For dry beans, after the pods dry and begin to split open, pull up mature plants and hang in a dry place until all of the pods split.

Pest Control
- Rotate bean plantings to a different place in the garden every year to reduce pest problems.
- Apply insecticide to control bean beetles, which eat holes in the leaves.

Recommended Selections
- For dry beans, dark red kidney matures in ninety-five days, great northern in ninety days.
- 'Blue Lake 274' and 'Tendercrop' are disease-resistant green bush beans.
- 'Fordhook 242' is a good large-seeded lima bean, while 'Baby Fordhook' and 'Eastland' are good choices for small-seeded limas.
- 'King of the Garden' is an outstanding lima pole bean.
- 'Blue Lake Pole' and 'Kentucky Blue' are excellent pole beans.

Beet
Beta vulgaris

A Versatile Vegetable with a Tasty Root and a Pungent Top

Garden beets are closely related to sugar beets and to Swiss chard. Beets originated in the maritime regions of Europe, and gardeners hybridized them in Germany and England in the middle of the sixteenth century. They are the main ingredient in borscht, but that certainly is not the only way to enjoy them. People love beets for both their globe-shaped roots and their leafy tops.

Top Reasons to Plant

○ Sweet, colorful roots
○ Tangy greens

Useful Hint

Beet seeds are actually dried fruits that each contain two or more seeds, so don't plant them too close together.

Planting Location

- Well-prepared, well-drained, loamy soil with lots of organic matter and a pH of 7 or higher
- Sun

Planting

- Apply 10-10-10 fertilizer at a rate of 1¹/₂ pounds per 100 square feet.
- Making sure the soil is thoroughly broken up, work it into a fine-textured seedbed.
- Sow seeds a month before the last expected spring frost.
- Make successive plantings about every three weeks until midsummer for a continuous supply of fresh beets.
- Place seeds an inch apart, and allow 12 to 15 inches between rows.
- Cover seeds with ¹/₂ inch of fine soil.
- Keep the seedbed moist.
- When seedlings are large enough to handle, thin to 1 to 3 inches apart.

Watering

- Provide an inch of water each week if there isn't that much rain.

Fertilizing

- No additional fertilizer is needed beyond bed preparation.

Suggestions for Vigorous Growth

- Hoe or pull weeds.

Easy Tip

Wait to thin beets until plants are 3 inches tall; then cook the thinned ones as greens.

Harvesting

- Cut leaves as needed from the tops when plants are 6 inches high, and use them as you would spinach.
- Harvest roots when they are 1¹/₂ inches in diameter—beets more than 3 inches in diameter are tough and woody.
- Dig late-season beets and store them in boxes of sand in a cool place, such as a garage, or in plastic bags with air holes—but don't let them freeze.

Pest Control

- Beets may be affected by leaf spots, leaf miners, or root maggots—consult your Extension Agent for controls.

Recommended Selections

- 'Avenger' is excellent for greens.
- 'Pacemaker III' matures early—in only fifty days.
- 'Ruby Queen' is top quality.
- 'Sweetheart' has tops good for greens.
- 'Bull's Blood', an antique variety, features deep-red tops.
- 'Burpee's Golden' is a yellow beet.
- 'Green Top Bunching' is outstanding for greens.

Broccoli

Brassica oleracea Cymosa group

A Favorite Vegetable Good Cooked or Raw

Broccoli grows along the coasts of Europe from Denmark to France. Although it has been cultivated for five thousand years, broccoli was developed from other cole crops as a specific crop quite late and has been popular in this country only since the 1930s. This vegetable, grown for its compact cluster—or head—of flower buds, is picked before the flower buds begin to open.

Top Reasons to Plant

○ Delicious heads of unopened flower buds
○ Tolerates partial shade
○ Withstands cold weather
○ Needs little care

Useful Hint

Secondary broccoli heads that develop between the bases of the leaves and the stem can be harvested for several weeks after the central head is cut.

Planting Location
- Well-drained, fertile soil with lots of organic matter
- Sun or partial shade

Planting
- Work 10-10-10 fertilizer at a rate of $1^1/_2$ pounds per 100 square feet of garden into the soil before planting.
- Sow seeds indoors about eight weeks before the last expected frost, and grow plants under lights or in a greenhouse.
- *Or* purchase transplants at the garden center.
- Put transplants in the garden three weeks before the last expected frost
- Space plants 18 inches apart, with 3 feet between rows.
- Set plants at the same depth they were growing in the container.

Watering
- Provide an inch of water each week if there hasn't been that much rain.

Fertilizing
- Side-dress with 10-10-10 fertilizer when the plants are about half-grown—10 to 12 inches tall.

Suggestions for Vigorous Growth
- No special care is required.

Easy Tip

For best results, plant broccoli early and harvest it before hot weather arrives, replacing it with a second crop for fall.

Harvesting
- Cut heads with a sharp knife, leaving about 6 inches of stem attached, while heads are still compact and before any flower buds open.
- Allow side shoots to develop for continuous production.
- Flowers on heads continue developing after harvest, so keep them in the refrigerator and use as quickly as possible.

Pest Control
- Cabbage worms can be prevented with a biological control spray or dust.
- Root and stem diseases may occur unless plantings of broccoli and other cole crops (Brussels sprouts, cabbage, collards) are rotated into different parts of the garden each year.

Recommended Selections
- 'Green Comet' produces early and tolerates heat.
- 'Premium Crop' has a good extended harvest.
- 'Romanesco' features spiraling chartreuse heads.

Cabbage

Brassica oleracea Capitata group

One of the Oldest and Best-Known Vegetables

Cabbage is a cole crop, a member of the mustard family, Brassicaceae. It's one of our oldest recorded vegetables, mentioned in literature three thousand years ago. Cabbage is easy to grow and will be much sweeter than what you find at the grocery. It's the main ingredient in cole slaw, which becomes a gourmet delight with garden-fresh produce. Cooked cabbage is also excellent, especially when stuffed with a savory mixture.

Top Reasons to Plant

- ○ Excellent raw or cooked
- ○ Tastier than grocery cabbage
- ○ Easy to grow
- ○ Tolerates light shade

Useful Hint

When buying transplants at the garden center, make sure they have a good green color, are short and compact, and have no pests.

Planting Location
- Well-prepared, well-drained soil
- Sun or partial shade

Planting
- Start seeds indoors under lights about eight weeks before the last expected frost.
- Apply 10-10-10 fertilizer at a rate of 1½ pounds per 100 square feet of garden; till the soil well.
- Set plants into the garden about two weeks before the last expected frost.
- Space plants 12 to 18 inches apart with 24 inches between rows.
- Put plants at the same depth they were growing in containers.
- Water with transplant solution.
- For a fall crop, direct-seed in midsummer.
- Sow seeds 3 inches apart and ½ inch deep.
- Thin seedlings to spacing noted for transplants.

Watering
- Provide an inch of water each week if there isn't that much rain.

Fertilizing
- Side-dress plants with 10-10-10 fertilizer when they are about half grown.

Suggestions for Vigorous Growth
- Do not plant cabbage where broccoli, Brussels sprouts, or collards were within the past year—root and stem disease pathogens may still be in the soil.

Easy Tip
Since the cabbage will be harvested and out of the garden by early summer, plan for a fall crop or follow it with a different vegetable.

- Keep cabbage watered properly—without sufficient water, cabbage heads crack as they develop.

Harvesting
- Cut just below the head with a sharp knife.
- Some varieties produce a second crop of small heads.
- Use as soon as possible to take advantage of peak freshness.
- Store fall-harvested cabbages for months at 40 degrees Fahrenheit in the refrigerator, wrapping them well so they won't dry out.

Pest Control
- Prevent infestations of cabbage worms with a biological spray or dust.

Recommended Selections
- 'Ruby Ball', a red cabbage, resists cracking.
- 'Savoy Express' is the earliest of the savoy (wrinkled leaf) types.
- 'Savoy Queen' tolerates heat.
- 'Dynamo' is a reliable, smooth green cabbage.
- 'King Cole' has large, firm 8-pound heads.

Carrot

Daucus carota var. *sativus*

A Bright-Orange Root Vegetable with Crunch

These vegetables with their bright-orange roots may not appeal to the youngest family members, and it seems that early peoples may have shared the youngsters' sentiments. The ancients probably cultivated carrots but not as a common food plant. Nevertheless, carrots have managed to gain popularity with a lot of folks since those early days. Most of the modern varieties come from those developed in France in the early 1800s.

Top Reasons to Plant

○ Crunchy, sweet taste
○ Long season of harvest
○ Tolerates cold weather

Useful Hint

The long varieties of carrots prefer sandy soils; the shorter or half-long varieties produce the best quality in gardens with heavy soils.

Planting Location

- Deeply prepared, well-drained, fertile soil
- Sun

Planting

- Apply 10-10-10 fertilizer at a rate of 1^1/$_2$ pounds per 100 square feet of garden, and work the soil into a fine seedbed.
- Sow seeds in mid- to late winter or just as soon as the soil is workable.
- Resow every two or three weeks for a continuous supply of carrots.
- Sow three seeds per inch with 12 to 15 inches between rows.
- Cover seeds with ^{1}/$_4$ inch of fine soil.
- Keep the seedbed moist.
- Thin seedlings to one plant every 2 inches.

Watering

- Provide an inch of water each week if there isn't that much rain.

Fertilizing

- No fertilizer is needed beyond that used for the bed preparation.

Suggestions for Vigorous Growth

- Keep weeds under control to avoid competition for water and nutrients.
- Prevent green shoulders—which aren't tasty—by cultivating a little loose soil over the roots as they begin to swell.

Harvesting

- Pull carrots when they are at least ^{1}/$_2$ inch in diameter.
- Carrots left in the ground continue increasing in size.

Easy Tip

A freeze does not harm carrots—in fact, it may make them sweeter.

- Expect the spring seeding to produce for three or four weeks.
- Leave the fall crop in the ground until a killing frost or later—if the crop is heavily mulched to prevent the ground from freezing.
- Dig late-season carrots, and store them in pits or boxes of sand in a cool place just above freezing temperatures, such as a garage.

Pest Control

- If soil-borne maggots become a problem, drench the soil with an appropriate insecticide using label directions—while planting seeds.

Recommended Selections

- 'Short 'n Sweet' has 4-inch roots and produces well in poor soils.
- 'Danvers Half Long' has 6- to 8-inch long roots.
- 'Scarlet Nantes' is the standard for high-quality—6-inch roots, bright orange, and sweet.
- 'Red-Cored Chantenay' and 'Royal Chantenay' work well in heavy soils.
- 'Thumbelina', a small, round carrot, is excellent for poor or shallow soils and for containers.

Collards

Brassica oleracea Acephala group

A Traditional Southern Vegetable That Always Produces

This cool-season leafy vegetable is a super cold-hardy member of the cabbage family. Collards tolerate both warm and cold temperatures better than cabbage. Because the plants can cope with our fickle weather, collards have long been a traditional Southern favorite and a staple of Southern cooking— sometimes the only thing in the garden to eat during the coldest part of winter!

Top Reasons to Plant

○ Tasty greens
○ Produces in winter and spring
○ Withstands cold and heat

Useful Hint

Collards do well in partial shade, but their leaves are larger and floppier, and the flavor milder.

Planting Location
• Well-drained, fertile soil
• Sun or partial shade

Planting
• Apply 10-10-10 fertilizer at a rate of 1$^1/_2$ pounds per 100 square feet of garden; till well into the soil.
• Plant in midsummer for fall and winter harvest, direct-seeding into the garden.
• Plant in late winter for spring and early summer harvest, using purchased transplants.
• Space transplants 12 to 18 inches apart with 30 inches between rows.
• Set plants at the same depth they were growing in the container.
• Water with a transplant solution.

Watering
• Provide an inch of water each week if there isn't that much rain.

Fertilizing
• No fertilizer is needed beyond that used for the original bed preparation.

Suggestions for Vigorous Growth
• No special care is required.

Easy Tip
When buying transplants, look for plants that are short and compact, have good green color, and are free of pests.

Harvesting
• Cut outer leaves as they reach full size.
• For tender inner leaves, blanch them by tying the outer leaves to block the sun from the inner ones.

Pest Control
• Prevent cabbage worms with a biological spray or dust.
• Eliminate stem and root diseases by avoiding planting where cabbage, collards, Brussels sprouts, or broccoli were planted in the past year.

Recommended Selections
• 'Blue Max' has a heavy yield.
• 'HiCrop' maintains excellent flavor in hot weather.
• 'Georgia', an old-time favorite, sweetens with the frost.

Corn

Zea mays var. *rugosa*

A Favorite Vegetable with Unsurpassed Taste Fresh from the Garden

This native crop is even more American than apple pie. Because sweet corn converts its sugar to starch rapidly upon harvest, old-time gardeners say that to enjoy the "sweetest" sweet corn, plant the patch close to the kitchen; when the corn is ready for harvest, start the pot of water boiling, and just as it reaches a full boil, pick the corn. Husk it as you run to the kitchen, then pop it into the pot.

Top Reasons to Plant

○ Wonderful flavor when just picked
○ Easy to grow
○ Can be interplanted with beans or pumpkins

Useful Hint

Three types of hybrid sweet corn are currently available—standard, sugar enhanced, and supersweet—but the sugar enhanced (SE) types are the best choice for the home garden.

Planting Location
- Well-drained, fertile soil
- Sun

Planting
- Apply 10-10-10 fertilizer at a rate of 1^1/$_2$ pounds per 100 square feet of garden, and mix it thoroughly into the soil.
- Sow seeds ^{1}/$_2$ inch deep in cool soils early in spring.
- Sow seeds 1^1/$_2$ inches deep in warm soils later in the season.
- Space seeds 9 inches apart in rows, with 24 to 36 inches between rows.
- Plant three or more rows of each variety side by side to ensure pollination.
- If growing different varieties, prevent cross-pollination by planting the varieties several yards apart with other crops in between.
- Continue planting every two weeks or when previous plantings have three leaves.

Watering
- Provide an inch of water each week if there isn't that much rain.
- Water is especially vital once the silks begin to dry.

Fertilizing
- Side-dress plants when they are a foot tall; use 10-10-10 fertilizer at the rate of 1 pound per 100 square feet of garden.

Suggestions for Vigorous Growth
- Control weeds by hoeing rows until the corn is tall enough to shade out weeds.

Easy Tip
Most corn plants are bred to produce only two ears per plant, so be sure to plant enough for your family's needs.

Harvesting
- Break off ears as soon as they're filled out and the kernels are milky inside—usually about twenty days after silks appear.
- Keep the corn cool, and use it as quickly as possible.

Pest Control
- Corn earworm is the most common pest—apply an appropriate insecticide to the silks as the pollen is being shed.
- Smut disease causes fungus to grow out of corn ears—plant resistant varieties.

Recommended Selections
- 'Peaches and Cream' is a popular bicolor.
- 'Seneca Dawn', a bicolor, bears early, is vigorous, and has excellent quality.
- 'Spring Snow' is a very early white.
- 'Sugar Snow', white and very sweet, is good in early cool weather.
- 'Champ' is an excellent, early yellow.
- 'Tuxedo' is highly recommended as disease resistant and vigorous, with excellent quality.
- 'Silver Queen', a popular standard white (not sugar enhanced), resists diseases well.
- 'Golden Bantam', an excellent old variety (not sugar enhanced), features a rich flavor.

Cucumber
Cucumis sativus

A Fresh or Pickled Treat with Mild Flavor

Vine crops closely related to squashes, pumpkins, and melons, cucumbers are warm-season plants known for their refreshingly mild fruits. Many kinds of cucumbers have been developed. Some are short; others are long and curved. Burpless types are never bitter. Like most vine crops, cucumbers can take up a lot of room. If that's a concern, look for the bush types, which take up less space and can even be grown in pots.

Top Reasons to Plant

○ Tasty, refreshing fruits
○ Large yield
○ Long season of harvest
○ Bush types take less space

Useful Hint

Like all vining crops, cucumbers have male and female flowers—male flowers do not produce fruit, so don't be concerned if flowers fall off before any cucumbers form.

Planting Location
- Well-drained, fertile soil
- Sun or light shade

Planting
- Apply 10-10-10 fertilizer at a rate of 1½ pounds per 100 square feet of garden, and mix it thoroughly into the soil.
- Start seeds indoors under lights on the average date of the last frost.
- *Or* sow seeds outdoors after all danger of frost has passed.
- Set transplants in the garden after all danger of frost has passed.
- Place six seeds or set two or three transplants in hills about 36 inches apart.
- Set plants at the same depth they were growing.
- Thin seedlings to two or three per hill once they are large enough to handle.
- Provide a trellis, strings, or a fence to support the vining types.

Watering
- Provide an inch of water each week if there isn't that much rain.

Fertilizing
- No fertilizer is needed after initial bed preparation.

Suggestions for Vigorous Growth
- Protect plants with row covers until vining begins.

Easy Tip
Be careful not to harm the tiny roots when transplanting cucumbers—they don't tolerate root injuries.

Harvesting
- Pick cucumbers when they are mature and before they yellow.

Pest Control
- Cucumber beetles eat and infect plants with bacterial wilt—which kills the plants about the time they begin setting fruit; use either row covers or an appropriate insecticide until plants begin vining.
- Cucumber mosaic, a virus, may cause misshapen, lumpy cucumbers—grow resistant varieties and control aphids (which carry the virus) with an appropriate insecticide.

Recommended Selections
- 'Bush Pickle' is a pickling type good for containers.
- 'Bush Crop' features delicious cukes on dwarf bushes.
- 'Fanfare' is a tasty, disease-resistant bush type.
- 'Salad Bush' has excellent disease resistance and produces 8-inch cukes on compact plants.
- 'Burpless' is the original burpless, vining type, with no bitterness.
- 'Straight 8' is a longtime favorite vining type.

English Pea

Pisum species

A Flavorful Treat When Fresh from the Garden

Peas are definitely cool-season plants, so intolerant of hot weather they quit producing when it arrives. "Picking the vines" as the peas develop in your garden is a sure way to have the best-tasting vegetables on your kitchen table. Gardeners grow peas for the immature, edible pods (sugar or snow peas), for the edible pods with immature seeds (snap peas), and for the mature seeds (English peas), which are shelled out for use.

○ Top Reasons to Plant

- ○ Delicious picked fresh
- ○ Bears early in season
- ○ Few pests
- ○ Easy to grow

Useful Hint

Peas derive their nitrogen from the air and do not need nitrogen fertilizers.

Planting Location
- Well-drained, fertile soil that dries out early in spring
- Sun or partial shade

Planting
- Apply 5-20-20 fertilizer at a rate of 1^1/$_2$ pounds per 100 square feet of garden, and mix it thoroughly into the soil.
- Prepare the soil in fall for early spring planting.
- Sow seeds 1 inch deep and 1 inch apart in rows 12 to 18 inches apart.
- Thin seedlings to 8 to 10 inches apart.
- Provide support for vining types.

Watering
- Peas need water only during a dry spring—provide an inch of water every ten days if there isn't that much rain.

Fertilizing
- No fertilizer is needed after initial bed preparation.

Suggestions for Vigorous Growth
- Give vining types—most sugar and snap peas are vining—support to conserve space, make picking easier, and keep the peas from getting muddy.
- Support the plants with "pea sticks"— small branches 2 to 4 feet long stuck in the ground along the rows.
- Biodegradable netting also works well as a support.

Easy Tip

By preparing the soil in the fall, you can sow the seeds at the earliest opportunity in the spring without having to wait to till the soil.

Harvesting
- Pick English peas when they are full sized and before they begin to dry— pods should be green, not turning tan.
- Pick snap peas when the pods are full sized and before the seeds mature.
- Pick sugar peas when the pods are fully formed but before the seeds begin developing.

Pest Control
- Root rot may be a problem in heavy clay soils during wet winters.

Recommended Selections
- 'Little Marvel' is an old standard English pea.
- 'Mr. Big', an English pea, needs no support.
- 'Sugar Daddy' is a stringless snap pea.
- 'Sugar Snap' is the classic vining snap pea.
- 'Dwarf Gray Sugar' is a tall sugar pea.
- 'Snowbird', a sugar pea, bears in clusters.

Garlic
Allium sativum

A Healthy Vegetable with a Pungent Flavor

Garlic consists of a cluster of small bulblets called cloves covered in a papery wrapper. It's an ancient vegetable, native to the Mediterranean. The Romans fed it to their slaves and soldiers because they believed it imparted extra strength, but they themselves despised its odor. Health benefits are attributed to garlic today, and it's a common item in health food stores. It is used in all types of cooking—especially European and Asian.

Top Reasons to Plant

○ Stores well
○ Many varieties available
○ Easy to grow

Useful Hint

Try both softneck and hardneck garlic to determine which you prefer—a huge selection of types is available for this trendy vegetable.

Planting Location
- Well-prepared, well-drained, fertile soil
- Sun

Planting
- Apply 10-10-10 fertilizer at a rate of 3 pounds per 100 square feet of garden, and mix it thoroughly into the soil.
- Work the soil into a fine seedbed with no clods or rocks.
- In fall, plant cloves 2 inches deep and 4 inches apart in rows 1 foot apart.

Watering
- Provide an inch of water each week if there isn't that much rain.

Fertilizing
- No fertilizer is needed after initial bed preparation.

Suggestions for Vigorous Growth
- Keep weeds under control—garlic won't shade them out.
- If flower heads begin developing in spring or early summer, snip them off to force energy into bulb production.

Harvesting
- Harvest when most of the leaves have turned yellow, usually early summer—do not wait for all leaves to yellow.
- If garlic is left in the ground too long, its papery covering deteriorates.
- Dig garlic in the morning during dry weather.
- Let the bulbs dry where they are in the garden until the afternoon.
- Collect the bulbs and spread them on screens or slats where they can cure for two or three weeks.

Easy Tip
For straight necks on bulbs, set the pointed ends of cloves up.

- After the bulbs have cured, brush off as much soil as possible and cut off the tops.
- *Or* braid the tops together and hang bunches in a dry place.
- Do not peel or wash the bulbs.

Pest Control
- If onion maggots are present in the soil, water the bulbs with the appropriate insecticide mixed in.

Recommended Selections
- Hardneck garlic (*Allium sativum* subsp. *ophioscorodon*) produces five to nine cloves per head in a single circle around a central woody stem. There are many types with high-quality flavor, but they have short- to medium-range storage properties. 'Purple Italian Easy Peel' has a rich, spicy flavor and a clean, fresh taste. 'Spanish Roja' has the flavor most garlic lovers prefer.
- Softneck garlic (*Allium sativum* subsp. *sativum*) produces six to eighteen cloves in several layers around a soft central stem. It has the best storage qualities and is the type to grow for garlic braids. 'Chinese Pink' is very early, maturing four to six weeks before most types. 'Sicilian Gold', an heirloom garlic brought from Sicily in the 1920s, has robust flavor.

Lettuce

Lactuca sativa

A Cool-Weather Vegetable That's Easy to Grow

No other salad crop is grown or used in such large quantities as lettuce. It's a cool-weather crop that can be grown in spring or fall. With hot weather, it becomes bitter and develops a tall seed stalk. Leaf, romaine, and butterhead or Bibb lettuce are commonly grown in home gardens. Lettuce germinates quickly and can be eaten very young, so it's an excellent choice when gardening with impatient children.

Top Reasons to Plant

- Fresh, tasty greens in early spring
- Easy to grow
- Good in containers
- Withstands cold weather

Useful Hint

Lettuce plants have shallow roots and are easily uprooted, so be very careful when pulling or hoeing weeds around them.

Planting Location
- Very well-drained, fertile soil
- Sun or partial shade (in hot weather)
- Containers

Planting
- Apply 10-10-10 fertilizer at a rate of 1½ pounds per 100 square feet of garden, and mix it thoroughly into the soil.
- For earliest production, use transplants, either homegrown or purchased.
- Sow seed indoors under lights—eight weeks before the last expected frost for head lettuce, and two weeks for leaf lettuce.
- Set out transplants three or four weeks before the last expected frost.
- Space head lettuce transplants 12 inches apart with 12 to 18 inches between rows.
- Space leaf lettuce transplants 4 to 6 inches apart with 6 inches between rows.
- Sow seeds of leaf lettuce outdoors as soon as the soil can be worked.
- Seed lettuce in triple rows (three closely spaced rows) 12 inches apart, then thin the leaf types to 4 to 6 inches apart.
- Plant every two or three weeks during spring.
- Begin planting again in August and September for fall and winter crops.

Watering
- Provide an inch of water each week if there isn't that much rain.

Fertilizing
- No fertilizer is needed after initial bed preparation.

Easy Tip
Lettuce picked in hot weather is bitter, so wash and store it in the refrigerator a few days—it will lose the bitterness.

Suggestions for Vigorous Growth
- Control weeds by careful hoeing or pulling.

Harvesting
- Snip off outer leaves as soon as they are large enough to use.
- As full plants become large enough to use, harvest every other one, leaving more room for the others.
- Harvest head, Bibb, and romaine lettuce when the heads are full sized.

Pest Control
- Control insects by keeping plants well spaced and harvested as they mature.
- Aphids may appear—spray the undersides of leaves with insecticidal soap and wash leaves well before eating.

Recommended Selections
- 'Buttercrunch', a Bibb lettuce, tolerates high temperatures.
- 'Summertime', a head lettuce, is slow to bolt.
- 'Black-seeded Simpson' is an early green leaf lettuce.
- 'Oak Leaf', a green leaf lettuce, does well in hot weather.
- 'Red Sails' is a slow-bolting, red leaf lettuce.
- 'Paris Island Cos' is a romaine lettuce that's slow to bolt.

Muskmelon

Cucumis melo Reticulatus group

Whether Called Cantaloupes or Muskmelons, These Fruits Are Sweet and Juicy

Muskmelons are vine crops, closely related to cucumbers, squashes, and pumpkins. These hot-weather plants with sweet, juicy fruit are commonly called cantaloupes, especially the small, smooth, round ones. Muskmelons, as well as honeydews and Crenshaws, two other summer melons, need a long, hot season to develop. Like most vine crops, muskmelons can occupy a lot of room, which may make them unrealistic in small gardens unless they're grown on trellises.

Top Reasons to Plant

○ Luscious, sweet fruit
○ Thrives in heat
○ May be grown on a trellis or fence

Useful Hint

Female muskmelon flowers are pollinated by bees that have visited male flowers. In cold, dark, wet weather when few bees roam, pollinate melons by hand. Clip a male flower and dust pollen on the pistils of the female flowers.

Planting Location
- Well-drained, fertile soil
- Sun

Planting
- Apply 10-10-10 fertilizer at a rate of 1¹/₂ pounds per 100 square feet of garden, and mix it thoroughly into the soil.
- Start seeds indoors under lights a week before the last expected frost.
- Set out started or purchased plants or sow seed directly in the garden after all danger of frost has passed.
- Sow seeds an inch deep in hills 3 feet apart.
- *Or* set two or three transplants in hills 3 feet apart.
- Set plants at the same depth they were growing.

Watering
- Provide an inch of water each week if there isn't that much rain.

Fertilizing
- No fertilizer is needed after initial bed preparation.

Suggestions for Vigorous Growth
- Train vining types on a trellis strong enough to support the melons—each melon may weigh 2 pounds, and there may be several on one vine.
- To provide additional support for fruits, use a little net or cloth parachute tied securely to the trellis or fence under each melon.
- Put row covers over plants until vining begins.

Easy Tip

Muskmelons need warm soil—about 70 degrees Fahrenheit—to develop and may rot off if the weather is cool and wet, so don't rush to get them into the garden in spring.

Harvesting
- Pick melons when they are ripe—when the rind changes from green to tan between the webbing on the surface, the fruit smells sweet, and a small crack appears next to where the stem is attached to the melon.
- Melons do not continue ripening once picked—they become softer but not sweeter.

Pest Control
- Cucumber beetles infect plants with bacterial wilt—which kills the plants about the time they begin fruiting; use row covers or spray with an appropriate insecticide.
- Protect foliage from diseases with an appropriate fungicide.

Recommended Selections
- 'Honeybush' is a sweet, nonvining hybrid.
- 'Limelight' is a sweet honeydew.
- 'Ambrosia', a vining melon too soft to ship, is the sweetest muskmelon.
- 'Magnifisweet', a vining type, rivals 'Ambrosia' in flavor.
- 'Harper Hybrid', a vining type, resists diseases well.

Okra

Abelmoschus esculentus

A Southern Classic with Succulent Green Pods

Okra, a relative of hollyhock and hibiscus, hails from the hottest parts of Africa. Gardeners grow the tall, leafy plants for their immature fruit pods or seed pods, which they use to thicken soups and stews and to cook as vegetables. Okra is what makes gumbo...gumbo! And what Southern buffet doesn't include a heaping helping of sliced, fried okra and a side of spicy pickled okra?

Top Reasons to Plant

○ Green pods with many uses
○ Thrives in heat
○ Needs little care
○ Long production season

Useful Hint

Experienced gardeners recommend soaking the seeds for exactly five minutes in pure chlorine bleach, rinsing the seeds three times, then planting them—they'll sprout the very next day!

Planting Location
- Well-drained, fertile soil
- Sun

Planting
- Apply 10-10-10 fertilizer at a rate of 1$^1/_2$ pounds per 100 square feet of garden, and mix it thoroughly into the soil.
- Seeds sprout slowly—soak them overnight to speed them up.
- Start seeds under lights indoors in late March, and set transplants out after all danger of frost has passed and the soil is warm.
- *Or* sow seed in the garden a week or so after all danger of frost has passed.
- Sow seeds in rows at least 3 feet apart.
- Thin plants to one every 12 inches.
- Set transplants at the same depth they were growing—take care not to damage the roots.
- Water in transplants with a transplant solution.

Watering
- Provide an inch of water each week if there isn't that much rain.

Fertilizing
- No fertilizer is needed after initial bed preparation.

Suggestions for Vigorous Growth
- Remove weeds by hoeing or pulling.

Easy Tip
Put these large, tall (up to 5- or 6-foot) plants where they won't shade out smaller plants.

Harvesting
- Using a knife or shears, remove pods when they are about 3 inches long and still tender.
- Cut pods every few days so the plant doesn't become woody.
- Wear long sleeves and gloves while harvesting—okra plants cause a rash on many people.
- To stimulate production, remove any overripe pods.
- Plants produce until the frost kills them.
- Use okra within a day or two of harvest.

Pest Control
- Few pests or diseases bother this plant—other than pod rot in hot, humid weather.
- Ants may feast on the sweet, sticky sap on the pods and flowers, but usually do no damage.

Recommended Selections
- 'Burgundy' has red pods.
- 'Cajun Delight' is early and attractive enough for the flower garden—if you avoid pesticide sprays that aren't for edible crops.
- 'Cowhorn' is tall with long, tender pods.
- 'Dwarf Green' is small with ribbed pods.
- 'White Velvet' is a prolific 5-foot plant with spineless pods.

Onion
Allium cepa

A Useful Vegetable That Belongs in Every Garden

Onions are one of the oldest crops in human history. The Old Testament describes them as one of the items the Israelites longed for during their long sojourn in the desert. Gardeners grow these members of the lily family for the immature green bunching onions, often called scallions, or for the mature dry bulbs. Onions are so easy to grow and so useful in the kitchen that they should be in every garden.

Top Reasons to Plant

- Staple in the kitchen
- Stores well
- Withstands cold weather
- Easy to grow

Useful Hint

Some onions form bulbs when days are short, others when days are long—Vidalia onions, a short-day type grown in winter, don't store as long because of their higher moisture content.

Planting Location
- Well-prepared, well-drained soil
- Sun

Planting
- Apply 10-10-10 fertilizer at a rate of 1¹/₂ pounds per 100 square feet of garden, and mix it thoroughly into the soil.
- Plant onion "sets" (tiny onion bulbs grown the previous season) as soon as the soil can be worked in mid- to late winter.
- Space sets 1 inch apart for green onions and 3 inches apart for dry onions.
- For dry onions, barely push the sets into the soil surface.
- For green onions, place sets 2 or 3 inches deep to develop long white stems.

Watering
- Provide an inch of water each week if there isn't that much rain.

Fertilizing
- Side-dress with 10-10-10 fertilizer when plants are about 12 inches tall.

Suggestions for Vigorous Growth
- Since onions have shallow roots, be careful as you pull or hoe weeds.
- Bulbs begin forming when the days get long—about fifteen hours; the size of the dry onion is determined by the size of the tops.

Harvesting
- Harvest green onions when the stems are pencil-sized.
- Pull any dry onions that form flower stalks and use them immediately—they do not store well.

Easy Tip
Onions may be grown from seeds sown directly in the garden or from seedling transplants called "stick-outs," but the easiest way to start them for the home garden is from sets.

- When tops begin to yellow and fall over, pull them to one side with the back of a rake.
- Do not crush the tops or the bulbs stop developing.
- Pull dry onions when all the tops have fallen, preferably in the morning during dry weather.
- Let the onions dry in the garden until the afternoon.
- Then spread them on screens or slats to cure for two or three weeks.
- Once the onions cure, knock off as much dirt as possible and cut the dry tops to about 1¹/₂ inches.
- Do not peel or wash the bulbs.
- Store onions in mesh bags or wire baskets in a dry, cool place, and they'll last all winter.

Pest Control
- If onion maggots are present in the soil, mix the appropriate insecticide in water and drench the soil when planting.

Recommended Selections
- 'Walla Walla Sweet' is a mild, long-day onion.
- 'Stuttgarter' is a popular, long-day onion.
- 'Southport White Globe' is a good slicer and a long-day onion.
- 'Texas 1015' is a very sweet, short-day onion, a bit sweeter than 'Vidalia'.

Peanut
Arachis hypogaea

A Fun Vegetable to Grow with Kids

Peanuts, sometimes called goober peas, are among the richest vegetables for oil content. They're divided into three general categories: *Spanish* (bunch) types produce nuts in clusters close to the main stem; *runner* types produce nuts scattered along their low-growing branches from tip to base; and *Virginia* types can be either runner or bunch. Virginia and runner types, mostly low-growing plants with usually two large seeds per pod, are the best producers for most gardens.

Top Reasons to Plant

- Fun to harvest
- Easy to grow
- Requires little care
- Interesting growth habit

Useful Hint

Peanuts grow in a unique way. When the single-stem, bush plants are mature, their low-growing branches produce yellow pealike flowers, from which pegs grow into the soil. Pods of nuts form in the ground from the ends of the pegs.

Planting Location
- Coarse-textured, sandy, fertile soil
- Sun

Planting
- Add lime to the soil at planting to increase both alkalinity and calcium content.
- Where peanuts or Southern peas weren't grown the year before, mix a fresh commercial peanut inoculant with the seeds immediately before planting.
- Use $1/2$ pound of seed per 100 feet of row.
- Remove seeds still in pods, being careful not to damage the seed coat or split the seed.
- Place seeds 2 or 3 inches apart on a wide, slightly raised bed with rows 2 feet apart, and cover them with $1^1/2$ to 2 inches of coarse soil.

Watering
- Soak the plants weekly during vigorous flowering and when pegs are entering the ground.
- *Do not water as harvest approaches,* or you'll risk seeds sprouting.

Fertilizing
- No fertilizer is needed after initial bed preparation.

Suggestions for Vigorous Growth
- Control weeds early on, but don't throw soil up to the plants during cultivation—that can cause stem diseases and bury the flowers.
- As the crop grows, cultivate by hand.
- When plants begin to flower and peg, lightly sprinkle lime over the rows to add calcium.

Easy Tip
All peanuts need at least four months until they are ready to be harvested.

Harvesting
- About two months after the plants bloom, the leaves begin to yellow.
- Dig up a few peanuts, and check the inner hulls.
- When most inner hulls are brown, dig the entire plants using a turning fork, being careful to break off as few pods as possible.
- Freshly dug peanuts are excellent boiled.
- For dry peanuts, move the plants to a warm, airy place for two to three weeks to finish curing before pulling the nuts from the plants.

Pest Control
- Caterpillars, aphids, and grubs may appear—if they're affecting the plants, ask your Extension Agent about controls.

Recommended Selections
- 'Florigiant', a Virginia type, is large when mature.
- 'Florunner' is a commonly grown runner type.
- 'Valencia', a popular small-seeded variety, has three or four seeds per pod.

Pepper

Capsicum species

A Big Vegetable Family with a Variety of Uses

The most familiar peppers are the bells—red, purple-lilac, yellow, and orange. These are generally mild and can be used as green peppers or allowed to ripen to one of the other colors. Hot peppers are usually called chilies, and the intensity of the heat and the flavor vary tremendously. Peppers and chilies can be bell-shaped, round, pointed, or slender, but most chilies are long and slim.

Top Reasons to Plant

○ Tasty fruits with variety of uses
○ Attractive plants
○ Easy to grow

Useful Hint

Peppers' heat, measured in Scoville units, ranges from the tolerable jalapenos at a respectable 3,000 to 5,000 Scoville units to the frighteningly hot habaneros at a staggering 285,000 Scoville units.

Planting Location
- Well-drained, fertile soil
- Sun

Planting
- Start seeds indoors under lights about two weeks before the last expected frost.
- *Or* buy transplants at the garden center.
- Apply 10-10-10 fertilizer at a rate of 1$^{1}/_{2}$ pounds per 100 square feet of garden, and mix it thoroughly into the soil.
- Place plants in the garden when all danger of frost has passed.
- Space plants 10 inches apart, with 18 to 24 inches between rows.
- Set plants at the same depth they were growing in containers.
- Water in with a transplanting solution.

Watering
- Provide an inch of water each week if there isn't that much rain.

Fertilizing
- Side-dress plants with 10-10-10 fertilizer when they have set fruit.

Suggestions for Vigorous Growth
- To promote pollination—which may be prevented by weather that's too hot, too cold, or too calm—tap the flowers with a pencil in the early morning to shake pollen from the flowers onto the pistil.

Harvesting
- Cut off sweet peppers at any size for green peppers.
- Let the new, brightly colored varieties

Easy Tip
Peppers are warm-weather plants, so don't be in a hurry to put them in the garden before the soil warms up— they'll just sit there and sulk.

mature—the flavor improves after ripening.
- Unless the recipe calls for green chilies, cut off hot peppers when they are red-ripe.
- Harvesting with a sharp knife or shears is better than pulling peppers off, which may break the plants.

Pest Control
- Avoid verticillium and fusarium wilts by planting disease-resistant varieties.
- Control any foliar diseases, if serious, with an appropriate fungicide.
- If aphids or mites appear, treat plants with insecticidal soap.
- Catfacing (malformed fruit) is due to poor pollination.

Recommended Selections
- 'Big Chili' is an Anaheim type hot pepper.
- 'Habanero' is blistering hot.
- 'TAM Jalapeno' isn't quite as hot as the usual jalapeno.
- 'Valencia', a late, orange sweet pepper, is excellent in salads.
- 'Giant Macaroni', an excellent, disease-resistant pepper, turns red when mature.
- 'Canary' is a fresh yellow sweet pepper.
- 'Lilac Bell' is lavender, turning red when mature.

Potato
Solanum tuberosum

America's Favorite Vegetable

In some parts of the world, potatoes are the main source of carbohydrates and are critical to the well-being of the citizenry. In the U.S., they're popular as snacks, chips, fries, and side dishes in many forms. Potatoes aren't fattening in and of themselves, as many people believe—the calories and fat come from the grease in which they're cooked or the sour cream and butter piled onto them.

Top Reasons to Plant

- Fun to grow
- Stores well
- Many varieties available
- Tasty new potatoes hard to find in stores

Useful Hint

Don't be in a rush to plant potatoes—if the soil is too wet and cold, the plants won't grow, and the seed pieces may rot.

Planting Location
- Well-drained, well-tilled soil with lots of organic matter
- Sun

Planting
- Apply 10-10-10 fertilizer at a rate of 1½ pounds per 100 square feet of garden, and mix it thoroughly into the soil.
- Purchase certified seed potatoes from a reliable outlet.
- Plant the seed potatoes three or four weeks before the last expected frost.
- Space the seed potatoes 12 to 15 inches apart with 24 inches between rows.
- Plant them 2 to 3 inches deep with the eyes up, then cover gently to avoid breaking off any sprouts.

Watering
- Provide an inch of water each week if there isn't that much rain.

Fertilizing
- No fertilizer is needed after initial bed preparation.

Suggestions for Vigorous Growth
- When sprouts are about 6 inches high, begin hilling soil around them by pulling soil from spaces between rows.
- Hills eventually should be about 6 inches high and 12 inches wide.

Harvesting
- About ten weeks after planting, flowers should appear, indicating the small "new" potatoes are ready.
- When vines begin to yellow, dig the potatoes as soon as possible to avoid damage by insects or diseases.

Easy Tip
In soil that's very heavy, rocky, shallow, or poorly drained, set the seed pieces firmly into the soil surface, then cover them loosely with 6 inches of clean straw—the potatoes will root into the soil, but the tubers will form at the soil surface.

- Carefully lift potatoes with a fork or spade.
- Spread potatoes on the ground for a couple of hours to dry.
- Do not wash potatoes before storing them.
- Put potatoes in a dark, warm place to cure for a week or so.

Pest Control
- Protect these plants from leaf hoppers, potato beetles, and flea beetles by using floating row covers or an appropriate insecticide.
- Avoid diseases by not planting potatoes where either they or other members of their family (peppers, tomatoes, eggplants) were planted the year before.
- Scab, a common disease, causes a rough surface on the tuber—buy scab-resistant varieties.

Recommended Selections
- 'Red Pontiac', a red potato, does well in heavy soil.
- 'Green Mountain', an heirloom white potato, produces many misshapen tubers that make the best-tasting baked potatoes ever.
- 'Yukon Gold' is a yellow potato with moist, flavorful flesh.

Pumpkin
Cucurbita species

A Favorite Vegetable for Pies and Jack-o'-Lanterns

Pumpkins are much loved decorations for the fall, but many people grow these warm-season vine crops for their flavorful flesh and for their seeds, too. Actually, pumpkins are winter squashes, picked when they're fully colored and mature. They take up a lot of space, but can be underplanted among the corn as the Native Americans did, where they'll flourish and provide the classic fall look intertwined with the brown corn stalks.

Top Reasons to Plant

○ Fruit for baking
○ Seeds for munching
○ Jack-o'-Lanterns for carving

Useful Hint

If your garden has restricted space, grow smaller-fruited vining types of pumpkins on supports or grow bush types in beds or containers.

Planting Location
• Well-drained, fertile soil
• Sun

Planting
• Apply 10-10-10 fertilizer at a rate of
  1^1/$_2$ pounds per 100 square feet of
  garden, and mix it thoroughly into
  the soil.
• For vining types, sow six seeds or
  carefully set two or three transplant
  seedlings in hills about 5 feet apart
  with rows 10 feet apart.
• Set transplants at the same depth they
  were growing.
• Thin seedlings to two or three per hill
  when they're large enough to handle.
• For bush types, space plants
  3 feet apart.
• For dwarf types, use one plant per
  container in 5-gallon buckets or
  half barrels.

Watering
• Provide an inch of water each week if
  there isn't that much rain.

Fertilizing
• Side-dress plants with nitrogen at
  half the normal rate when the vines
  have almost covered the ground,
  being careful to rinse the fertilizer
  off the leaves.

Suggestions for Vigorous Growth
• No special care is needed.

Harvesting
• Using shears, cut handles 3 or
  4 inches from the fruit.

Easy Tip
Sow seeds before July 1 to ensure you
have pumpkins for Halloween carving.

• Harvest pumpkins when they have full
  color (no green on them).
• Keep pumpkins in a warm place
  (80 degrees Fahrenheit) after harvest
  to harden them off.

Pest Control
• Squash vine borers may be a problem,
  burrowing into the vines and eventually
  killing them—control these by applying
  an appropriate insecticide to the stems
  of the plants every two weeks, starting
  when the plants begin to vine.
• Control cucumber beetles and squash
  bugs with appropriate insecticides.
• Apply insecticides carefully after sunset
  but before dark to avoid harming the
  bees, essential for pollination.

Recommended Selections
• 'Bushkin' and 'Spirit' are semibush
  Jack-o'-Lantern pumpkins.
• 'Connecticut Field' is the standard
  among large pumpkins.
• 'Rouge Vif d'Etamps', the original
  "Cinderella's carriage" pumpkin—
  features a beautiful, flat, deep-orange
  fruit with pronounced lobes.
• 'Jack Be Little' is a 3-inch pumpkin.
• 'Snack Jack' is bred for seeds.
• 'Trick or Treat' is excellent for carving.
• 'New England Pie' is the standard
  among pie pumpkins.

Radish
Raphanus sativus

A Fast-Growing Garnish Great for Kids

Radishes are fast-growing, cool-weather vegetables. They grow anywhere with some sun and moist, fertile soil. They do well in gardens, pots, planters, flower beds, and cold frames. Fresh radishes make tasty garnishes, hors d'oeuvres, or additions to salads. Because they are among the first things to plant in spring and develop so quickly, radishes are excellent vegetables to use to introduce children to gardening.

Top Reasons to Plant

- Grows to maturity in twenty-five days
- Prefers cool weather
- Tolerates partial shade
- Easy to grow

Useful Hint

Fall radishes are larger, crisper, and hotter than the spring crop—plus they can be left in the ground longer since they don't bolt.

Planting Location
- Moist, fertile soil
- Sun or partial shade
- Containers

Planting
- Apply 10-10-10 fertilizer at a rate of 1½ pounds per 100 square feet of garden, and mix it thoroughly into the soil.
- Work the soil into a fine seedbed.
- Sow seeds as soon as the soil can be worked in spring or in late summer or fall for a fall or winter crop.
- Place seeds about three per inch in rows 8 to 10 inches apart.
- Cover seeds with ¼ inch of fine soil.
- Thin spring radishes to 1 inch apart.
- Thin fall or winter radishes to 3 or 4 inches apart.

Watering
- Provide an inch of water each week if there isn't that much rain.

Fertilizing
- No fertilizer is needed after initial bed preparation.

Suggestions for Vigorous Growth
- Hoe or pull weeds, especially while seedlings are small.

Easy Tip

Choose a well-drained part of the garden for radishes—it will dry out more quickly in spring and allow early planting.

Harvesting
- Pull spring radishes at about 1 inch in size and winter radishes at 3 inches.

Pest Control
- No serious pests or diseases trouble this plant.

Recommended Selections
- 'Easter Egg' is a spring radish in various colors.
- 'Champion', 'Cherry Belle', and 'Early Scarlet Globe' are red spring radishes.
- 'Burpee White' and 'Snow Belle' are white spring radishes.
- 'Icicle' is a long, slim, white radish
- 'Black Spanish', a white winter radish, has black skin.
- 'Tama', a white, daikon type of winter radish, is 18 inches long.

Southern Peas
Vigna unguiculata

A Southern Favorite with Lots of Variety

To a Southerner, peas mean black-eyed, not English. Also known as field peas and cowpeas, Southern peas—high-protein bean relatives— come in a huge array of pod and seed colors, sizes, shapes, and flavors, and they grow on vines or bushes. Small kinds are sometimes called lady peas, and other popular types are called crowders, creams, black-eyes, pinkeyes, purple hulls, and silver skins. They can be cooked fresh, canned, made into dips, or dried and stored.

Top Reasons to Plant

- Some varieties are difficult to find at groceries
- Very tasty when fresh
- Stores and dries well
- Good soil-enriching cover crop
- Long season of yield

Useful Hint

Southern peas won't tolerate cool soils, so wait to plant them until at least two weeks after the last expected frost.

Planting Location
- Well-drained, fertile, slightly acidic soil
- Sun

Planting
- Plant seeds 1 inch deep in clay soils and 2 inches deep in sandy soils.
- Place seeds 4 to 6 inches apart in rows 3 feet apart.
- Thin seedlings to 6 to 12 inches apart.

Watering
- Southern peas tolerate drought well, so water only in extreme dry spells.

Fertilizing
- Too much nitrogen fertilizer increases plant size but reduces yield—so use fertilizer sparingly.

Suggestions for Vigorous Growth
- No special care is needed.

Harvesting
- Pick peas as pods begin to change color.
- Pick purple hull types when hulls are 50 percent colored.
- For dried peas, let the last flush ripen and dry on the vine, then pick and store them.

Easy Tip
Southern peas take nitrogen from the air, so they need little or no nitrogen fertilizer.

Pest Control
- Stink bugs and aphids may appear—consult your Extension Agent for controls.

Recommended Selections
- Robust vines with small seeds, field peas produce a dark liquid when cooked.
- Crowder peas have starchy seeds "crowded" into pods.
- Cream peas grow on smaller, almost bushy plants and have light-colored seeds that are light when cooked—'Zipper Cream' is a good variety.
- Black-eyed peas have a dark "eye"—'California Blackeye' is the number 1 variety.
- Purple hull peas, including pinkeyes, have pods that turn purple or burgundy when mature—'Mississippi Purple' and 'Pinkeye Purple Hull' are productive varieties.

Spinach

Spinacia oleracea

A Versatile Leafy Vegetable Adored by Popeye

Even Popeye can't persuade many youngsters to like spinach due to their unfortunate early experiences with boiled spinach, but most adults eventually appreciate its diversity in such treats as salads, quiches, pizzas, crepes, and omelets. Spinach is a cool-weather crop that can produce in spring or fall. It matures when little else is coming from the garden, but it also stops growing and sets seed as soon as the weather warms.

Top Reasons to Plant

- Produces early in season
- Prefers cold weather
- Tolerates partial shade

Useful Hint

Since spinach will be harvested and out of the garden by midsummer, plan to replace it with a fall crop.

Planting Location
- Well-drained, moist, fertile soil
- Sun or partial shade

Planting
- Apply 10-10-10 fertilizer at a rate of 1½ pounds per 100 square feet of garden, and mix it thoroughly into the soil.
- Direct-seed into the garden as soon as the soil can be worked.
- Make several plantings seven to ten days apart to spread out the harvest.
- Sow seeds in rows 12 inches apart, and thin to 6 inches apart.
- *Or* sow seeds indoors about two months before the last expected frost and grow under lights as transplants.
- *Or* purchase transplants at the garden center.
- Set out transplants three or four weeks before the last expected frost.
- Space transplants 6 to 8 inches apart with 12 inches between rows.
- Set plants at the same depth they were growing.

Watering
- Provide an inch of water each week if there isn't that much rain.

Fertilizing
- No fertilizer is needed after initial bed preparation.

Suggestions for Vigorous Growth
- Weed by careful hoeing or pulling while weeds are small—spinach plants have shallow roots and are easily pulled up.

Easy Tip
Some gardeners prepare the soil in the fall and broadcast spinach seed over the frozen ground, where it sprouts as soon as the weather warms at all.

Harvesting
- Snip off outer leaves as soon as they're large enough to use.
- When plants are large enough to harvest, cut every other one off at the base, leaving room for the others to continue growing.
- As soon as plants begin to bolt (send up seed stalks), harvest all remaining leaves.

Pest Control
- If aphids appear, spray with insecticidal soap, and wash spinach carefully before eating.
- Leaf miners may be controlled with row covers.
- Plant resistant varieties to avoid disease problems.

Recommended Selections
- 'Avon' has crinkled leaves and good heat tolerance.
- 'Bloomsdale Long Standing' is an old favorite with crinkled leaves.
- 'Catalina', an upright smooth-leaf spinach, is slow to bolt.
- 'Giant Noble' has smooth leaves and tolerates heat.

Squash

Cucurbita species

A Vining Vegetable with Flavorful Flesh

Squashes are warm-season vine crops with flavorful flesh. They're divided into summer squash, grown for the immature fruit, and winter squash, harvested when mature. Squash can take a lot of room, so be prepared. Vining types spread 10 feet or more but can be grown on trellises with adequate support for the heavy fruits. In recent years, bush types have been developed that require much less space.

Top Reasons to Plant

○ Prolific production
○ Summer and winter types available
○ Loves hot weather
○ Winter types store well

Useful Hint

Male flowers—those with straight stems—are produced first and fall off; it's the female flowers—those with tiny squashes below the petals—that produce fruit.

Planting Location
• Well-drained, fertile soil
• Sun or partial shade
• Containers (bush types only)

Planting
• Apply 10-10-10 fertilizer at a rate of 1^1/$_2$ pounds per 100 square feet of garden, and mix it thoroughly into the soil.
• Sow six seeds or set two or three transplants in hills about 5 feet apart with rows 10 feet apart after all danger of frost has passed.
• Thin seedlings to two or three per hill when they are large enough to handle.
• Pinch off rather than pull extra plants.
• Put one dwarf bush type in a 5-gallon bucket, half-barrel, or similar container with drainage holes.

Watering
• Provide an inch of water each week if there isn't that much rain.

Fertilizing
• Side-dress with nitrogen when vines have almost covered the ground, rinsing any fertilizer off the leaves.

Suggestions for Vigorous Growth
• No special care is needed.

Harvesting
• Pick elongated types of summer squash when they are 6 to 8 inches long and less than 2 inches in diameter.
• Pick scalloped (patty pan) types when they are about 4 inches in diameter.
• Harvest every day when plants are producing heavily to encourage more production.

Easy Tip

Don't rush squash into the garden in spring—the plants need warm weather to develop and may rot if the weather is cool and wet.

• Pick winter squashes when they've developed full color and the rinds are hard enough that you can't pierce them with your fingernail.
• Cut handles 4 to 5 inches long on winter squash.
• Store winter squashes in a warm place after harvest to harden them off, then keep them in a dry place at 50 to 60 degrees Fahrenheit.

Pest Control
• Squash vine borers burrow into vines, eventually killing them—consult your Extension Agent about appropriate controls.
• Squash bugs damage fruits so that they rot in winter storage—control them with an appropriate insecticide.
• Cucumber beetles can be controlled with an appropriate insecticide.

Recommended Selections
• 'Chefini' is an excellent green zucchini.
• 'Scallopini' is a productive scalloped (patty pan) squash.
• 'Early Yellow Summer' is a classic crookneck summer squash.
• 'Table Queen' is a standard, dark-green acorn (winter) squash.
• 'Early Butternut' is a flavorful, early butternut (winter) squash.

Sweet Potato

Ipomoea batatas

A Tasty, Healthy Vegetable with Lots of Uses

Because of their need for long, warm growing conditions, sweet potatoes are often thought of as exclusively Southern. Their vigorous, ground-hugging vines are ornamental with lobed leaves (including some popular colorful varieties such as 'Blackie' and 'Margarita'). The tubers, depending on variety, have a rich or mellow taste, and the textures range from creamy or dry to dense and even stringy. Nothing beats a sweet potato pie or fried sweet potatoes!

Top Reasons to Plant

- Luscious tubers
- Easy to grow
- Attractive foliage
- Drought tolerant

Useful Hint

To reduce insect and disease build-up, rotate planting sites for sweet potatoes from year to year.

Planting Location
• Loose, well-drained soil
• Sunny and hot

Planting
• Do not plant until at least two weeks after the last frost.
• Purchase fresh vine cuttings (called slips) in spring.
• Bury slips in warm soil, 1 foot apart in rows 3 feet apart, or in mounds 4 feet apart.
• Set slips so only their stem tips and two or three leaves are left exposed.

Watering
• Do not overwater—a slow deep soaking every three or four weeks is adequate.

Fertilizing
• Do not overfertilize—at most, side-dress lightly with a low-nitrogen, high-potash fertilizer a month after planting.

Suggestions for Vigorous Growth
• No special care is needed.

Harvesting
• Dig roots when the soil is fairly dry and the air is warm.
• Early harvesting results in many small roots—late harvesting produces jumbo roots but possibly with cold damage or cracked from heavy rain.
• Handle freshly dug roots carefully.

Easy Tip

Sweet potatoes take four months or more from setting the plants until harvest.

• Do not wash after digging.
• Move the dug tubers quickly into shade to prevent sun scald.
• Allow to cure for several days.
• Store in a warm, humid place above 50 degrees Fahrenheit.

Pest Control
• Soil rot and soil insects may be problems, but there are no current adequate controls except regular crop rotation.

Recommended Selections
• 'Centennial' is the leading variety—the tubers have deep-orange, soft flesh, and the plant tolerates clay soils.
• 'Jewel' is the queen of sweet potatoes, with moist, soft, yellow flesh when baked.
• 'Nancy Hall', a popular old variety, features light-yellow flesh that's juicy and sweet when baked.

Tomato

Lycopersicon esculentum

Everybody's Favorite Garden Vegetable

The flavor of a newly picked tomato from your garden is unsurpassed. Plants are either *determinate* (bushes grow to a certain size and set all of the fruit about the same time) or *indeterminate* (fruit clusters form along a vining stem that continues growing all season). There are also some new *semideterminate* types that stay short but still produce all season. And of course, there are dwarf varieties suitable for containers.

Top Reasons to Plant

○ Fabulous fresh fruit
○ Heavy producer
○ Many varieties available

Useful Hint

Selecting tomatoes to grow may be difficult—there are over four thousand varieties in an incredible range of sizes, shapes, colors, growth habits, and maturity dates.

Planting Location
- Well-prepared, moist, well-drained soil with lots of organic matter
- Sun

Planting
- Apply 5-20-20 fertilizer at a rate of 1 pound per 100 square feet of garden—or 10-10-10 at a rate of $1/2$ pound per 100 square feet—and mix it thoroughly into the soil.
- Set out transplants after all danger of frost has passed.
- Space plants 2 to 3 feet apart depending on type.
- Place plants at the same depth they were growing in containers.
- Water in with transplant solution.

Watering
- Provide an inch of water each week if there isn't that much rain.

Fertilizing
- After plants have tomatoes about the size of golf balls, side-dress with 10-10-10 at the rate of 1 pound per 100 square feet, and repeat every three to four weeks until harvest has ended.

Suggestions for Vigorous Growth
- Mulch plants after soil warms up to maintain even moisture.
- Assist pollination—tap flower clusters with a pencil in the early morning to shake pollen from the flowers on to the pistil.
- Provide support to keep plants off the ground.
- Tie indeterminate types to stakes, then prune to a single stem by pinching off shoots that develop at each leaf axil.

Easy Tip
If tomato transplants are leggy, plant them on their sides, and lightly cover the long stems with soil—the tips of the stems quickly turn upward, and the buried stems sprout new roots.

- Grow determinate and semideterminate types in cages made of concrete reinforcing wire.

Harvesting
- Pick tomatoes as they ripen but before they're overripe and begin to split.
- Store at room temperature—quality diminishes rapidly if tomatoes are refrigerated.

Pest Control
- Verticillium and fusarium wilts and a disease called yellows affect tomatoes; plant disease-resistant varieties.
- Control foliar diseases with maneb fungicide.
- If aphids and mites appear, spray with insecticidal soap.
- For caterpillars and beetles, use Sevin®.

Recommended Selections
- 'Early Girl' is the earliest of the full-sized tomatoes.
- 'Bradley' is very popular in Tennessee.
- 'Better Boy' is widely available.
- 'Patio Hybrid' has nearly normal-sized fruit on dwarf plants.
- 'Tiny Tim' is a good cherry type.
- 'Sweet 100' is a heavy-producing, very sweet salad tomato.
- 'Brandywine' is an excellent pink heirloom tomato.

Watermelon

Citrullus lanatus

A Summertime Treat Beloved by All

Summertime celebrations would be incomplete without watermelons. As is the case with other summer melons, watermelons need a long, hot season to develop. They are vine crops, and like most vine crops, watermelons take a lot of room. If you're reluctant to try them because you have restricted space, plant smaller-fruited kinds, often called icebox watermelons. They can be grown on trellises if there's adequate support for the fruits.

Top Reasons to Plant

○ Delicious sweet fruits
○ Small types for restricted spaces
○ Bush types excellent for home gardens

Useful Hint

Pollination of watermelons is done by bees—if the weather discourages them, aid pollination by clipping a male flower (the one with a slender stem) and dusting the pollen from it onto the pistils of the female flowers (those with small watermelons under the petals).

Planting Location
- Well-drained, fertile soil
- Sun

Planting
- Start seeds indoors under lights in peat pots about a month before the expected last frost.
- Apply 10-10-10 fertilizer at a rate of 1½ pounds per 100 square feet of garden, and mix it thoroughly into the soil.
- Set out plants or sow seeds after all danger of frost has passed.
- Put two or three transplants or sow six seeds in hills about 36 inches apart.
- Set plants at the same depth they were growing.
- Thin seedlings to three per hill by snipping off unwanted plants.

Watering
- Provide an inch of water each week if there isn't that much rain.

Fertilizing
- No fertilizer is needed after initial bed preparation.

Suggestions for Vigorous Growth
- Black plastic mulch can get watermelons off to a good start since it traps the sun, warming the soil.
- Cut holes in the plastic with a knife or scissors.
- Plant seedlings in the holes.
- If space is an issue, grow melons vertically on a trellis or fence that's strongly supported.

Easy Tip
Watermelons can't stand any frost and love warm soil, so don't plant them until the weather is warm and settled.

- Place a little net or cloth parachute under each melon, and tie it securely to the trellis.

Harvesting
- Harvest melons when the bottom where it's lying on the ground is a golden yellow.
- The little curlicue where the melon attaches to the stem dries up as the melon ripens.
- As melons ripen, the skin becomes dull, rough, and hard enough that you can't pierce it with your fingernail.

Pest Control
- Cucumber beetles can be controlled with floating row covers or with an appropriate insecticide.

Recommended Selections
- 'Bush Sugar Baby', a bush type, produces early fruit.
- 'Sugar Baby' is a favorite icebox type.
- 'Cotton Candy' is a large seedless melon with red flesh.
- 'Queen of Hearts' is a mid-sized red seedless melon.
- 'Stone Mountain', a very large melon, offers rich, crisp, sweet, scarlet flesh.

FRUITS

Contents

Apple

Malus cultivars

A Classic Fruit for Any Back Yard

With the availability of dwarf apple trees, nearly any back yard can produce tasty apples. Standard-sized trees reach 30 feet or more, semidwarfs reach 15 to 20 feet, and dwarfs grow 7 to 10 feet. Minidwarfs can be kept to about 5 feet. If apples are high on your planting list, remember that without intensive pest control, you'll harvest cosmetically blemished fruit.

Top Reasons to Plant

○ Tart, crisp, or sweet fruit
○ Beautiful spring blooms

Useful Hint

Check with your nursery, garden center, or Extension Agent for pollinators for the apple you've chosen.

Planting Location
- Well-drained, fertile soil
- Sun

Planting
- Plant in fall after first frost or in early spring as soon as the soil is workable.
- Dig the hole twice as wide as the roots and at the same depth.
- For bare-root trees, spread the roots on the bottom of the hole and set the tree at the same depth it was growing.
- For container-grown trees, set the rootball at ground level.
- Backfill the hole with soil removed from it.
- Firm the soil around the roots.
- Water thoroughly.
- Stake dwarf trees permanently with a 4-foot post on the southwest side of the tree, 1 foot from the trunk.

Watering
- Provide an inch of water each week if there isn't that much rain.

Fertilizing
- If not growing $1^1/2$ to 2 feet each year, feed in spring with 10-10-10 fertilizer at the rate of $1^1/2$ pounds per 100 square feet.

Suggestions for Vigorous Growth
- Keep well mulched with 2 or 3 inches of organic mulch covering the entire area of the branch system and a few feet beyond.
- Prune annually in mid- to late winter to develop a central trunk with six to twenty horizontal branches in whorls around it.

Easy Tip
Spraying your apple trees can be kept to a minimum by following good cultural practices and by keeping the area under your tree clean.

- Thin the fruits between full bloom and four weeks after full bloom to space the fruits about 6 inches apart.
- After the tree is a mature size, prune it each winter to remove dead or damaged branches, water sprouts (vigorous vertical branches growing from the base of the tree or from branches), suckers at the base of the tree, and branches touching the ground.

Harvesting
- When apples develop their characteristic coloring, taste them for ripeness.
- Harvest immediately when ripe.

Pest Control
- A number of insects and diseases attack apple trees—consult your Extension Agent for a spray schedule for the pests and diseases in your area.

Recommended Selections
- 'Gala' is good for fresh eating and salads.
- 'Ozark Gold' is a yellow apple of excellent quality.
- 'Rome Beauty' is a red apple excellent for baking.
- 'Stayman' is a tasty, tart, all-purpose red apple.
- 'Granny Smith' is a yellow-green apple of excellent quality.

Blackberry

Rubus cultivars

Tasty Fruit for Eating Fresh and Making Pies and Preserves

Blackberries are brambles that grow on biennial canes developing from perennial roots. The canes grow vigorously the first year, fruit the second year, then die. Blackberries come in two types—upright and trailing. The upright varieties can be planted as a hedge, but the trailing types make long vines that need to be supported to keep the berries off the ground and to simplify harvesting.

Top Reasons to Plant

- Garden fresh berries
- Pretty spring blooms
- Useful as a hedge

Useful Hint

If any blackberry plants begin developing misshapen leaves, get rid of the plants immediately, and if the plants begin producing small berries, consider replacing all plants—these are signs of virus diseases that have no cure.

Planting Location
- Well-drained, fertile soil
- Full sun

Planting
- Buy certified, disease-free plants from a reliable garden center or nursery.
- Plant in fall after the first frost or in early spring as soon as the soil is workable.
- Space erect blackberries 2 feet apart in rows 8 to 10 feet apart.
- Space trailing blackberries 10 feet apart in rows 8 to 10 feet apart.
- Dig the planting hole the same diameter and depth as the root spread.
- Set bare-root or container plants at the same depth they were growing.
- Refill the hole with soil, and firm it around the roots.
- Water well.

Watering
- Provide an inch of water each week as fruit is ripening if there isn't that much rain.

Fertilizing
- For the first two years, feed the plant with 2 pounds of 10-10-10 fertilizer per 100 feet of row or $1/4$ pound per plant—in spring and again after harvest.
- After two years, feed with 4 pounds of 10-10-10 in spring or $1/2$ pound per plant in spring and again after harvest.

Suggestions for Vigorous Growth
- After planting, cut canes back to about 1 foot tall, and burn or otherwise dispose of prunings to prevent disease.
- Mulch well to conserve moisture and to discourage weeds.

Easy Tip
Blackberries are subject to verticillium wilt, so don't put them where other susceptible plants such as potatoes, tomatoes, or peppers have grown in the past five years.

- Train vining types on trellises or fences for easier care.
- In early spring, thin the canes of trailing blackberries to the best and largest eight to sixteen canes.
- In early spring, thin the canes of upright blackberries to the largest, most vigorous four or five canes.
- Cut back lateral canes to about 15 inches and pinch back new canes as they reach desired height.
- After fruiting is completed, remove all canes that bore fruit.

Harvesting
- Pick the berries as they ripen—color is the primary indicator of ripeness.

Pest Control
- A number of insects and diseases attack blackberries—consult your Extension Agent for a spray schedule for pests and diseases in your area.

Recommended Selections
- 'Arapaho' is an erect, thornless type with early-ripening fruit.
- 'Black Satin', a thornless trailing type, has good berry production.
- 'Kiowa' is a thorny, erect type with very large fruit over six weeks.

Blueberry
Vaccinium species

Delicious Fruit from a Decorative Bush

Cultivated blueberry production in Tennessee consists predominantly of the Northern highbush blueberry (*Vaccinium corymbosum*) and the rabbiteye blueberry (*Vaccinium ashei*), a native Southern blueberry. The Southern highbush blueberry is a relatively new type that's a hybrid between the Northern highbush and one or more native Southern blueberries. The Northern highbush is best suited for the colder parts of the state, while the rabbiteye and Southern highbush types do better in warmer areas.

Top Reasons to Plant

○ Fresh-picked berries
○ Ornamental plants
○ Few pests or diseases
○ Thrives in acidic soil

Useful Hint

Southern highbush and rabbiteye blueberries require cross-pollination by another cultivar of the same type and maturity time—Northern highbush types tend to be self-fertile, but produce better if cross-pollinated.

Planting Location
- Highly organic, well-drained, acidic soil with a pH of 4.5 to 5.6
- Sun

Planting
- Purchase vigorous, two-year-old plants.
- Plant in fall after the first frost or early spring as soon as the soil is workable.
- Have the soil tested before planting—if pH is 6.2 or higher, modify the soil to add acidity.
- Dig the planting hole twice as wide and not quite as deep as the roots.
- Space plants 6 feet apart in rows 8 feet apart.
- Set plants in holes 2 inches higher than they grew previously—poor drainage may cause root or crown rot.
- Replace half the soil, and fill the hole with water.
- After the water drains, fill the holes with the remaining soil.
- Water thoroughly.
- Mound soil over the exposed upper rootball.
- Mulch with 2 or 3 inches of shredded bark or compost.

Watering
- Provide an inch of water each week if there isn't that much rain.
- Irrigate with a soaker hose to avoid wetting the foliage and fruit.

Fertilizing
- Feed four weeks after planting with an organic fertilizer or cottonseed meal, following label directions.
- The next three years, apply fertilizer again in spring just before buds begin to swell.

Easy Tip

Plant a few blueberry bushes in your shrub border—they have pretty blooms, nice summer foliage, decorative berries, and gorgeous fall color.

- The fourth year, split the fertilizer application in two: half in early spring and half six weeks later.

Suggestions for Vigorous Growth
- Keep mulched with 2 or 3 inches of mulch year-round.
- Hoe out any weeds, being careful not to injure shallow blueberry roots.
- Plant flowers near blueberries to attract bees for pollination.

Harvesting
- Pick berries when they're fully blue in color and taste sweet.
- Several pickings may be needed at five-day intervals.

Pest Control
- Few insects or diseases trouble this plant.
- Birds can be troublesome—try "hawkeye" balloons or cover the plants with netting.
- Fence with chicken wire to deter rabbits.

Recommended Selections
- Different blueberry cultivars taste similar—select yours based on local availability, growing habit, and maturity times.

Fig

Ficus carica

Delectable Fruit from a Good-Looking Tree

Figs suffer winter damage in the colder parts of the state unless they're given protection. But their soft, luscious fruit, prized for fresh eating and preserves, make any trouble worthwhile. Figs prefer hot, dry summers and cool winters. Southern fig varieties don't need a pollinator, so one tree is just fine. The main crop occurs on the current season's growth, but after a mild winter, a small crop is produced on last year's twigs.

Top Reasons to Plant

○ Tasty fruit
○ Attractive ornamental tree
○ Tolerates variety of soils
○ Grows fast

Useful Hint

Place figs where they have room to grow—a space 15 feet wide and high is the minimum—heavy yearly pruning causes poor fruiting.

Planting Location
- Fertile, well-drained soil
- Sun

Planting
- Plant in spring as soon as the soil is workable.
- Dig the hole at least three times as wide as and the same depth as the rootball.
- Set the plant at the depth it grew previously.
- Refill the hole with soil from the hole.
- Water well.

Watering
- Provide an inch of water each week if there isn't that much rain, especially when the fruit is swelling.

Fertilizing
- Spread 3 cups of 8-8-8 fertilizer under the canopy of a well-established plant in March, May, and June—use half that amount for younger plants.

Suggestions for Vigorous Growth
- Keep grass away from underneath the plant—it competes for nutrients and water.
- If figs often suffer winter injury in your area, use only half the fertilizer recommended above.
- If plants grow well but don't fruit heavily, do not fertilize for six months.
- If pruning is necessary, do it in summer.

Easy Tip
In cold areas, plant figs on the south side of the house, and try to avoid early-morning and late-evening sunshine in winter.

- Remove tips of vertical spouts when they're 2 feet long.
- Encourage horizontal branches—they'll bear most of the fruit.

Harvesting
- Pick the fruit as soon as it ripens— June or July on last year's wood, September or October on this year's
- Ripe figs come off easily when lifted and bent back toward the branch.

Pest Control
- Few pests or diseases trouble this plant.
- Birds love figs, but many gardeners figure figs grow tall "so the birds can have the high ones, and I get the low ones"—the only sure protection is to cover the plants with netting.

Recommended Selections
- 'Brown Turkey' is hardy to 10 degrees Fahrenheit and produces some fruit even if frozen to the ground in winter.
- 'Celeste' has small fruit and is hardy to 0 degrees Fahrenheit.
- 'Kadota' has small or medium fruit with a rich, sweet flavor.

Grape

Vitis cultivars

A Heat-Loving Fruit on a Vine Casting Beautiful Shade

American and French hybrid bunch grapes can be grown in all parts of the state as long as you choose varieties adapted to your area. You can grow them in your garden as ornamentals or just for the fruit. Unfortunately, many are grown on arbors suited for decoration and for sitting under on a hot afternoon but which are inappropriate for managing the grapes. Keep that in mind as you choose a structure to support them.

Top Reasons to Plant

- Bunches of attractive, sweet fruit
- Beautiful foliage
- Loves hot weather
- Provides shade

Useful Hint

Proper pruning of grapes removes about 90 percent of the wood on a vine and is best done in very early spring to avoid lots of messy sap "bleeding" from the wounds—it isn't harmful but is painful to see.

Planting Location
- Well-drained soil that's not too fertile
- Sun

Planting
- Construct the support system you'll use.
- Plant in early spring as soon as the soil is workable.
- Space plants 10 feet apart along the support.
- Set plants at the same depth as at the nursery.
- Firm the soil, and water well.

Watering
- Water deeply during extended dry periods.

Fertilizing
- For young vines, apply $1/4$ cup of 10-10-10 fertilizer around each plant, beginning a month after planting.
- Repeat the above application every six weeks until mid-July.
- For two-year-old vines, double the first-year rate and feed at the same intervals.
- Bearing vines need $2^1/2$ pounds of 10-10-10 applied in March.

Suggestions for Vigorous Growth
- Immediately after planting, prune to a single stem with two buds.
- After new growth starts in spring, select the more vigorous cane, tie it to a stake, and remove the other cane.
- Let the cane grow until it reaches the top of the trellis, then pinch out the tip to induce branching—this will be the vine's trunk.
- Train the resulting two sprouts along the support.

Easy Tip
Hillsides are excellent for grapes, since cold air flows downward, reducing the chance of late-season frosts and drying foliage more quickly, making disease problems less likely.

- Select a shorter cane near each of the four arms, and prune it back to two buds, removing other sprouts along the trunk.
- Remove flowers or fruit clusters that develop during the second year.
- Once vines begin producing, prune every spring, selecting four moderately strong lateral branches from last year, pruning them back, and leaving six to ten buds on each—these will produce this year's fruit.
- Also select four smaller laterals, cutting them back to two buds each—these are renewal spurs for next year's laterals.

Harvesting
- Cut clusters in late summer to early fall.

Pest Control
- A number of insects and diseases attack grapes—check with your Extension Agent for a spraying schedule for pests and diseases in your area.

Recommended Selections
- 'Sunbelt', a blue grape, ripens more evenly than 'Concord'.
- 'Aurora', a white grape, is good for both eating fresh and making wine.
- 'Steuben', a red grape, is good for jelly and eating fresh.

Peach

Prunus persica

A Delectable Fruit That's Tough to Grow

Peach trees are challenging to grow in the South, even though Georgia is known as the Peach State and the Carolinas produce huge numbers each year. They are susceptible to several damaging diseases and insects. The flower buds are killed outright by winter temperatures of minus 10 degrees Fahrenheit. They are also easily killed by late-season frost. In addition, peaches must have a minimum number of chill hours each winter, so mild winters can cause crop failure.

Top Reasons to Plant

○ Delicious fruit
○ Beautiful spring blooms

Useful Hint

Peach trees on dwarf rootstock will spread 12 to 15 feet, and standard trees will be twice that size, so place your tree carefully to give it room to grow.

Planting Location
- Well-drained, fertile soil
- Sun
- Protected from winter wind

Planting
- Plant in spring after all danger of frost has passed.
- Dig the hole twice as wide as and as deep as the roots.
- For bare-root trees, spread the roots on the bottom of the hole and set the tree at the same depth it was growing.
- For container-grown trees, set the rootball at ground level.
- Backfill the hole halfway.
- Firm the soil around the roots.
- When the hole is half-filled, water thoroughly.
- After the water has drained, fill the hole with the remaining soil, and water again.

Watering
- Provide an inch of water each week if there isn't that much rain.

Fertilizing
- Feed young trees in April with 1 cup of 10-10-10 fertilizer, and with 1/2 cup in early June and again in early August.
- Beginning the second year, feed the tree every March with 1 cup of 10-10-10 per year of tree age to a maximum 10 cups for a mature tree; feed again in August with 1 cup of 10-10-10 per year of tree age to a maximum 4 cups for a mature tree.

Suggestions for Vigorous Growth
- Prune in spring to create a bowl-shaped tree with no central leader.

Easy Tip

Easy Tip

While peach trees are hardy, their blossoms are not—if you're planting on a slope, plant the trees where they're protected from the wind but not at the bottom of the hill where cold air will settle.

- Keep trees low and well thinned out.
- As trees age, they'll need heavier and heavier pruning.
- Thin the fruits between bloom and six weeks after bloom to one fruit every 6 inches.
- For containerized trees, move in winter to an area with temperatures between 10 and 40 degrees Fahrenheit.

Harvesting
- Pick the fruit when ripe or a few days earlier—peaches continue ripening after harvest.
- Taste is the best way to determine ripeness.

Pest Control
- Insects such as Japanese beetles, stink bugs, and aphids attack peaches, as do diseases such as leaf curl, scab, and brown rot—consult your Extension Agent for a spray schedule for insects and diseases in your area.

Recommended Selections
- 'Belle of Georgia' has white flesh and a free stone.
- 'Cresthaven' has yellow flesh and a free stone.
- 'Redhaven' and 'Surecrop' have yellow flesh and semifree stones.

Pear

Pyrus communis

A Late-Summer Fruit Dripping with Juice

Pears would be as plentiful as apples if it were not for the bacterial disease called fire blight. Most European and Asian pears are extremely susceptible to the disease. Pears can be grown successfully in home gardens, however, by selecting disease-resistant varieties and carefully pruning them to remove diseased branches. And well-grown pears, sweet and full of juice, are a true delight that many gardeners find worth the trouble.

Top Reasons to Plant

○ Juicy, sweet fruit
○ Beautiful spring blooms

Useful Hint

You'll need to plant two varieties of pears for cross-pollination, so check with your garden center, nursery, or Extension Agent about which varieties cross-pollinate the others.

Planting Location
- Well-drained soil
- Sun

Planting
- Plant October through November or in spring as soon as the soil is workable.
- Dig the hole twice as wide and as deep as the roots.
- For bare-root trees, spread the roots on the bottom of the hole and set the tree at the same depth it was growing.
- For container-grown trees, set the rootball at ground level.
- Backfill the hole halfway.
- When the hole is half-filled, water thoroughly.
- After the water has drained, fill the hole with the remaining soil, and water again.

Watering
- Provide an inch of water each week if there isn't that much rain.

Fertilizing
- If young trees are not growing $1^1/2$ feet per year, feed with 10-10-10 fertilizer at the rate of $1^1/2$ pounds per 100 square feet of ground beneath each tree.

Suggestions for Vigorous Growth
- Keep well mulched with 2 or 3 inches of organic mulch covering the entire area of the branch system.
- Prune annually in mid- to late winter to develop a central trunk with six to twenty horizontal branches in whorls around the trunk.
- Thin the fruits between full bloom and four weeks after full bloom to space the fruits about 6 inches apart.

Easy Tip

Pears grafted onto dwarf rootstock attain a height and spread of 8 to 12 feet and bear almost as much fruit as standard trees, which grow to twice their size.

- After the tree is a mature size, prune it each winter to remove dead or damaged branches, water sprouts, suckers at the base of the tree, and branches touching the ground.

Harvesting
- Pick pears before they're fully ripe— ripe pears are soft and especially attractive to yellow jackets and birds.

Pest Control
- Fire blight, a bacterial disease spread by bees in the spring, is the biggest enemy of pear trees.
- Remove all affected areas by cutting at least 6 inches below signs of the disease.
- Sterilize pruners with bleach or disinfectant before each cut.
- A number of insects and diseases attack pears—consult your Extension Agent for a spray schedule for insects and diseases common to your area.

Recommended Selections
- 'Orient' has high fire blight resistance and large fruit.
- 'Seckel' is very high quality and fire blight resistant.
- 'Shinseki', an Asian pear, matures early and has excellent flavor.

Plum

Prunus cultivars

An Excellent Fruit for the Backyard Orchard

Plums are an excellent addition to the backyard grower's orchard. The three major types are European (*Prunus domestica*), Oriental (*Prunus salicina*), and native American (*Prunus americana*). European plums aren't suited for backyard production. Native American types have extremely tough skin and poor flavor. Oriental types are the ones you see in supermarkets, and the best trees are hybrids between the Oriental trees and the native American types.

Top Reasons to Plant

○ Juicy, tart-sweet fruit
○ Beautiful spring blooms

Useful Hint

Plum trees may reach 20 feet in width, so plant them where there's room to walk around the tree when it matures.

Planting Location
- Well-drained soil
- Full sun

Planting
- Plant in spring after all danger of frost has passed.
- Dig the hole twice as wide and as deep as the roots.
- For bare-root trees, spread the roots on the bottom of the hole and set the tree at the same depth it was growing.
- For container-grown trees, set the rootball at ground level.
- Backfill the hole halfway.
- Firm the soil around the roots.
- When the hole is half-filled, water thoroughly.
- After the water has drained, fill the hole with the remaining soil, and water again.

Watering
- Provide an inch of water each week if there isn't that much rain.

Fertilizing
- Feed young trees in April with 1 cup of 10-10-10 fertilizer, and with $1/2$ cup in early June and again in early August.
- Beginning in the second year, feed the tree in March with 1 cup of 10-10-10 per year of tree age to a maximum 10 cups for a mature tree; feed again in August with 1 cup of 10-10-10 per year of tree age to a maximum 4 cups for a mature tree.

Suggestions for Vigorous Growth
- Prune in spring to create a bowl-shaped tree with no central leader.
- Keep trees low and thinned out well.

Easy Tip

Plant two varieties of plums for cross-pollination, and place the two trees within 10 to 100 feet of each other.

- As trees age, they'll need more and more pruning.
- Thin the fruits between bloom and four weeks after bloom to one fruit every 6 inches.

Harvesting
- Pick plums when they're fully ripe.
- The fruit continues to ripen after the full color appears, so taste to determine ripeness.
- Plums don't ripen all at the same time, so several pickings are necessary.
- Plums don't continue ripening after harvest, so don't pick them too early.

Pest Control
- Japanese beetles and aphids may attack plums, as may diseases such as brown rot and black knot—consult your Extension Agent for a spray schedule for pests and diseases common to your area.

Recommended Selections
- The A.U. series ('Amber', 'Homeside', 'Producer', 'Roadside', and 'Rubrum') are all good choices.
- 'Byrongold' does well in colder parts of the state.
- 'Ozark Premium' is cold hardy and bears extremely large fruit.
- 'Rubysweet' has excellent flavor.

Raspberry
Rubus cultivars

An Outstanding Treat Fresh from the Garden

Growing a few raspberries in your backyard is the best way to enjoy these beautiful, delicious fruits. They're easy to grow, and they're extremely productive. You'll have to do a lot of pruning, but the fruit is worth the effort. Raspberries grow from biennial canes that grow vigorously their first year, then produce fruit the next summer and die. The crowns are perennial, sending up new shoots every spring.

Top Reasons to Plant

○ Wonderful fruit
○ Easy to grow
○ Very productive

Useful Hint

Raspberries are much more attractive and easier to care for when they're trained in some manner to a support.

Planting Location
- Well-drained, fertile soil
- Sun

Planting
- Buy certified, disease-free plants from a reliable garden center or nursery.
- Plant in early spring as soon as the soil is workable.
- Plant in rows or along a trellis.
- Space erect raspberries 2 feet apart in rows 8 to 10 feet apart.
- Space trailing raspberries 10 feet apart in rows 8 to 10 feet apart.
- Dig the planting hole the same diameter and depth as the root spread.
- Set bare-root or container plants at the same depth they were growing.
- Refill the hole with soil, and firm it around the roots.
- Water well.

Watering
- Raspberries tolerate drought well, but provide an inch of water each week as the fruit is ripening if there isn't that much rain.

Fertilizing
- For the first two years, feed the plant with 2 pounds of 10-10-10 fertilizer per 100 feet of row or $1/4$ pound per plant in spring and again after harvest.
- After two years, feed with 4 pounds of 10-10-10 in spring or $1/2$ pound per plant in spring and again after harvest.

Suggestions for Vigorous Growth
- Wearing long sleeves and gloves, prune in early spring, removing all canes that are falling over or are less than pencil-sized; save only the largest canes.

Easy Tip
Be sure to leave enough room around the planting so you can mow and rototill each spring to control suckers.

- Leave one cane every foot in rows.
- Cut all canes back to 5 feet tall if plants are supported, 3 feet if not.
- As soon as fruiting ends, remove all canes that bore fruit.

Harvesting
- Pick the berries when they achieve full color.
- Berries deteriorate rapidly—pick them quickly, or the birds, squirrels, and insects will harvest them for you.

Pest Control
- If plantings deteriorate before the bushes are ten years old, they probably have a virus disease for which there's no cure—replace plantings that begin to consistently produce small berries.
- A number of insects and diseases attack raspberries—consult your Extension Agent for a spray schedule for pests and diseases common to your area.

Recommended Selections
- 'Dormanred' is trailing and bears fruit in spring—it does well in the state.
- 'Heritage' is erect and bears fruit in fall.
- 'Latham' is erect and bears fruit in early summer.

Strawberry

Fragaria cultivars

Succulent Fruit for Shortcake and Whipped Cream

Strawberries respond to good treatment and reward your time and effort with plenty of high-quality fruit. Neglect them, and the berry patch quickly deteriorates. Choose from three types of strawberries— June-bearing types that produce a heavy crop for two or three weeks in June; everbearing types that produce crops in June, midsummer, and fall; and day-neutral types that produce flowers and fruit all season. For fresh berries all summer, choose everbearing or day-neutral varieties.

Top Reasons to Plant

○ Terrific tasting berries
○ Long season of production possible
○ Ornamental

Useful Hint

The growing system described here is the "matted row" system. Mother plants are set out the first spring and flowers are removed with fruit production occurring in the second and third years from the runners produced the first year.

114

Planting Location
- Well-drained, fertile soil
- Sun

Planting
- Make the bed about 8 feet wide and 30 feet long for a family of four.
- About a week before planting, broadcast 5 pounds of 10-10-10 fertilizer over the bed, till in well, and smooth the bed.
- Measure out two rows 4 feet apart, with each row 2 feet from the edge of the bed.
- Set plants 2 feet apart in the rows, making sure the top of each crown is just above the soil line.
- Water well.

Watering
- Provide an inch of water each week if there isn't that amount of rain.

Fertilizing
- Feed a new bed with 4 pounds of 10-10-10 fertilizer in mid-June and again in late September.
- In late winter beginning the second year feed with 4 pounds of 10-10-10.
- In mid-July feed with 3 pounds of 10-10-10, and in mid- to late September feed with 4 pounds of 10-10-10.

Suggestions for Vigorous Growth
- Remove all flowers the first year.
- Keep the bed well weeded.
- Mulch the entire bed with a 1- to 2-inch layer of pine straw in late winter.
- Rake most of the straw off the tops of plants.
- After harvest, mow the leaves from the plants, making sure the mower setting

Easy Tip
To avoid disease problems, buy only certified virus-free plants.

is high enough not to damage plant crowns.
- Turn the soil so the strip of remaining plants is about 8 inches wide, saving mostly the young plants instead of the original mother plants.
- Till up about two-thirds of the plants, or you'll have too many the next year.
- Fertilize with 4 pounds of 10-10-10 and immediately irrigate with an inch of water.
- If the bed is still in good condition after two picking seasons, renovate it again for a third year.

Harvesting
- Pick berries when fully red—about thirty days after first bloom.
- Snap off berries with the cap and a small piece of stem attached.
- Do not let berries remain on plants when fully ripe, or the critters will harvest them for you.

Pest Control
- Few pests and diseases bother this plant—if you start with disease-free plants.

Recommended Selections
- 'Chandler', a high-yield June-bearer, has excellent flavor.
- 'Ozark Beauty' bears all season and is very productive.
- 'Gem' bears all season with a heavy yield.

Gardening Basics

Garden plants are divided into two main kinds, annuals and perennials. Annual plants start from seed, grow, flower, and produce a fruit and more seeds in one season. Tomatoes, lettuce, corn, and beans are examples of annuals. Perennial plants grow from seed, develop a plant for the first year or so, and then flower and produce fruit and seeds each year thereafter. Rhubarb, strawberries, and apple trees are examples of perennials. The first two are herbaceous perennials; that is, the tops die down every fall, but the plants grow again in spring. Trees are woody perennials; that is, only the leaves die, and the rest of the above-ground parts live from year to year.

A third kind of plant, a biennial, grows a rosette of foliage from seed the first year, produces a flower, fruit, and seed the second year, and then dies. Several biennials are grown as garden plants, but they are usually handled as annuals. The leaves or roots are used, and the plants are discarded after the first year before they bolt (flower). Parsley and carrots are biennials.

Parts of a Plant

Plants consist of above-ground parts and below-ground parts. Generally, everything above ground is a shoot, and below-ground parts are roots. There are some exceptions. Occasionally, roots develop above ground, such as aerial roots on wandering fig trees, philodendrons, or orchid plants; and some shoot parts, such as tubers or rhizomes, develop below ground. Roots anchor the plants, absorb water and fertilizer nutrients, and often store sugars and starches for use by the plants later. Above ground, stems not only transport water and nutrients but also support the leaves, flowers, and fruits. Some stems store sugars and starches as the roots do. Leaves photosynthesize to produce sugars, using water from the soil and carbon dioxide from the air.

Flowers produce seeds and fruits. Pollination of flowers by insects or by the wind causes seeds to begin to develop. Then fruits develop around the seeds. Some kinds of plants, such as the vines (squash and melon), have separate male and female flowers on the same plant. Male flowers have straight stems, while female flowers have tiny undeveloped fruits below the petals. Technically, many vegetables are really fruits. Any plant part that develops from a flower is a *fruit,* so tomatoes, zucchini, and pumpkins are fruits, just as apples and strawberries are fruits. Peas, beans, and corn are seeds that develop inside the fruits. *Vegetables* are the leaves, stems, or roots that we eat. Lettuce, asparagus, carrots, and potatoes are vegetables. Common usage has confused this distinction so that any plant part with a sweet taste is considered a fruit, and the rest are vegetables. Although a tomato or a sugar pea is a fruit, we commonly call it a vegetable. Is a pumpkin a fruit, or is it a vegetable? The answer is yes!

Soil Chemistry

The soil provides most of the fertilizer elements needed by plants, and productive soils generally have enough of the elements in forms available to plants. (Carbon, oxygen, and hydrogen come from the air and water.) The correct soil acidity and sufficient air and water are necessary for these elements to be available. The major elements (those needed in larger amounts by plants) are nitrogen, phosphorus, potassium, calcium, magnesium, and sulfur. Minor elements (those needed in smaller amounts) include iron, manganese, boron, zinc, copper, molybdenum, cobalt, and chlorine.

Testing Your Soil

Plants need adequate nutrients in order to grow properly. They receive nutrients from the soil, from rain, and from the fertilizer you add. You should test your soil every two to three years to determine which nutrients your plants require.

1. *Evaluate the Areas*

   Good gardeners notice when they have different soil types in different areas of their landscape. It is possible that you have the same soil throughout. It might be dark-brown sandy loam, gray sticky clay, or common red clay. If earth grading was done before your home was built, perhaps the front yard is one soil type and the backyard is different because the topsoil was moved from one place to another. Collect separate samples of soil from each of your soil types. After you have tested the soil, you can make decisions on how to fertilize each area properly.

2. *Collect the Sample*

   Use a clean trowel and a plastic bucket. In each soil area to be tested, take a deep, hearty scoop (a *plug*) of soil from ten randomly chosen spots scattered across the area. A plug should be 4 to 6 inches deep, so that soil from the plant root zone will be tested, not soil on top of the ground. Place the plugs in the bucket.

3. *Mix the Plugs*

   When ten plugs have been collected from an area, mix them together in the bucket. Remove stones, grass, worms, and other materials. Scoop out approximately two 8-ounce cups of soil. This is a representative sample of all of the soil in a particular area.

   Repeat steps 2 and 3 for each different soil area in your landscape. While you are at it, take soil samples from your lawn and flower beds, keeping each representative sample separate and labeled. Soil in which landscape plants are growing needs to be tested, too, just like the soil in your food-growing area.

4. *Test the Soil*

   * **Using a Commercial Testing Kit**

     Purchase a soil testing kit from a garden center. Read the directions carefully. If you do not understand them, ask a garden center employee or a gardening friend to explain them. Most kits require you to add chemicals to a small sample of soil and water and to wait for a color change. Once the color has developed, compare it to a color chart, which gives you an estimate of the nutrients available for your plants.

     Commercial kits are generally easy to use, but their results might not be as accurate as you would like. It takes a sharp eye to compare colors, and this comparison is made more difficult by the orange or gray color of native clay.

   * **Using a Laboratory**

     The most convenient and accurate soil testing laboratory is usually run by your university Extension Service. Your County Extension Office can give you details on how to bring a soil sample to it. There is a nominal charge, in the range of $4 to $8, for each sample.

     The laboratory will test your soil and send you a written report on the nutrients it contains. The acidity (pH) of the soil will also be noted. Fertilizer recommendations will be included, along with the amount of lime needed by your soil.

5. *Interpret the Results*

One of the most important results is the acidity (pH) of your soil. Add the recommended amount of lime before digging and planting your garden. The commercial kits will make general recommendations for the amount of fertilizer to use. The laboratory results will recommend amounts of specific fertilizers. Don't worry if you cannot find the exact fertilizer analysis mentioned in a soil test result. If 10-10-10 fertilizer is recommended, either 8-8-8 or 13-13-13 can be substituted as long as you use a bit more or a bit less, respectively, than the recommended amount of 10-10-10.

Organic Fertilizer Recommendations

Some gardeners prefer to use plant nutrients that come from natural sources: manure, compost, bloodmeal, fish emulsion, or bonemeal. Organic gardeners believe in feeding the soil and allowing the soil to feed their plants. Organic fertilizers add both plant nutrients and organic *amendments* to the soil. These organic amendments decompose to form organic *matter*. Organic matter is the "glue" that holds soil particles—sand, silt, and clay—together to build and improve soil structure.

A soil with good structure is a healthy soil. It holds water, and it has a good mix of oxygen and carbon dioxide and a thriving microbial population. Good arguments can be raised on both sides of the question of organic versus synthetic fertilizer sources, but no one disagrees that all plants need nutrients to thrive.

If you receive a soil test result that recommends synthetic fertilizers, there is no reason you can't convert it to an organic recommendation. The first step is to notice the synthetic fertilizer nutrient ratio. If a fertilizer such as 16-4-8 is recommended, the ratio is 4:1:2. Knowing this ratio allows you to combine organic fertilizers to approximate what your plants need.

Understanding the Numbers on a Fertilizer Bag

All fertilizers are required to list the amounts of plant nutrients they contain. A plant needs 3 major nutrients: nitrogen (N), phosphorus (P), and potassium (K). The numbers on a container of fertilizer denote the percentage of N, P, and K inside. For example, a bag of 5-10-15 has 5 percent nitrogen, 10 percent phosphorus, and 15 percent potassium. Thirty percent of the bag's content is plant food; the rest is an inert filler, such as clay.

What Is the Purpose of Plant Nutrients?

What Does Nitrogen Do?

Nitrogen promotes the growth of roots, stems, and leaves. An appropriate supply of nitrogen gives plants healthy dark-green foliage. Too much nitrogen can cause growth to be too rapid, causing the plant to grow tall and fall over. Excess nitrogen can also delay or prevent flower and fruit formation. It can make plants more susceptible to diseases and insect damage.

What Does Phosphorus Do?

Phosphorus is involved in storing plant energy. Plants store energy in their seeds, roots, and bark. Plants need adequate phosphorus in order to flower. Phosphorus is essential for flower, fruit, and seed production. Plants lacking sufficient phosphorus usually have purplish leaves, petioles, and stems. They grow slowly and mature very late.

What Does Potassium Do?

Potassium is important for the manufacture of carbohydrates (sugar and starch) by plants. When sufficient potassium is available, plants produce stiff, erect stems, and the plants are more disease resistant. When insufficient or excess potassium is in the soil, plants contain too much water, they are susceptible to cold injury, and their growth is reduced.

What Do Micronutrients Do?

Nitrogen, phosphorus, and potassium are called *macronutrients* because plants need them in significant amounts. Plants also need other nutrients in order to grow and remain healthy. Because smaller amounts of these nutrients are needed, they are called *micronutrients*.

Calcium (Ca), magnesium (Mg), iron (Fe), sulfur (S), and many other nutrients are needed in small amounts. A lack of calcium in tomatoes causes the condition known as blossom-end rot. A lack of iron can cause leaves to turn yellow.

Most soils have enough micronutrients to keep plants healthy. However, if your soil is very sandy or is all clay, micronutrients may be needed. The best way to supply micronutrients is by mixing manure, compost, or enriched fertilizer with your soil.

What Does Garden Lime Do?

Garden lime raises the pH of soil. A big factor in determining how much of a particular nutrient is available to a plant is the acidity or alkalinity of the soil in which the plant is growing. Southern soils tend to be acidic by nature. Regular applications of fertilizer acidify the soil even further.

Acid soil ties up many nutrients. They are less available to your plants, even though they are physically present in the soil. For this reason, lime is regularly applied to soil to counteract the soil's acidity and raise its pH.

What Is pH?

pH is a numerical measurement of a soil's acidity. The pH number scale ranges from 0.0 to 14.0. A pH number from 0.0 to 7.0 indicates acid conditions. A pH number from 7.0 to 14.0 indicates an alkaline soil. Most plants grow best when the soil pH is between 5.5 and 6.5. Some plants, such as blueberries and potatoes, tolerate more acidic soil than other plants and usually do not need to be limed.

Preparing a Bed

Just as newlyweds select a cozy bed to share each night, plants must be given a comfortable bed (of a completely different nature!) in which to grow. Preparing the bed is a simple but vital job. If you plant tomatoes in hard clay, they will never look like the picture on the gardening magazine cover. If you plant lettuce in sandy soil and full sunshine along the coast, you'll have nothing but bleached leaves by May.

Preparing a bed requires a bit of work, but it is a chore that will reward you and your plants for years to come. Plant roots need 3 things: oxygen, moisture, and nutrients. The magic ingredient that provides or enhances these 3 things is organic matter. Whether you use composted pine bark, animal manure, or compost that you make yourself, it is almost always a good idea to mix organic matter into your existing soil before you plant.

Adding the right amount is important too. A dusting of rotten leaves added to a bed does no good. Your goal should be to have a bed that is $1/3$ organic matter and $2/3$ existing soil.

Many gardeners find that preparing a bed 2 months before planting allows them to observe drainage patterns and to pluck persistent weeds. With that lead time they may correct any obvious problems. Here are the steps to follow:

1. *Use a shovel or rototiller to dig up the soil in the location you've chosen. Loosen the soil to a depth of 10 inches.*
2. *Thoroughly break up the big clods of earth. All clumps should be less than 1 inch in diameter. Discard rocks, roots, and weeds as you work.*
3. *Add a 2-inch layer of organic amendment such as compost, composted pine bark, or aged animal manure to the area you tilled. Mix it deeply and completely with the existing soil.*

Replacing Organic Matter

Summer heat and rainfall slowly cook away the organic matter in your garden soil. A few years after you worked so hard to make good planting beds, they will need another infusion of rich organic matter. This presents a problem if you have a bed of asparagus or a trellis of brambles that you don't intend to move. The best way to replenish organic matter is to add a 1-inch layer of composted manure on top of the soil each January. First rake away any mulch around your plants, add the manure, then cover with fresh mulch. When the soil warms, earthworms and other creatures will go to work tilling the soil without any more work on your part.

Composting

The best source of organic materials for your garden is homemade compost. Why is it better than the store-bought stuff? Because it's alive! Compost is full of tiny fungi, bacteria, and other creatures. These organisms can digest leaves, grass clippings, lettuce leaves, and wood chips. Euphemistically, we say they "break down" these items. In fact, they eat and then excrete organic materials. As anyone who has changed a baby diaper knows, that stuff is sticky. The sticky excreta of fungi and bacteria are made that way by a substance called *glomalin*. This glomalin glues together the tiny particles of clay in your soil. When tiny grains of soil become big soil granules, the soil becomes soft and loose. Sterilized cow manure can't do that. Composted wood fiber can't do that. Both are valuable soil amendments, but compost is best.

Composting is not rocket science. If you have a corner where 2 fences meet, pile your fall leaves there. In 6 months, you'll have compost. In fact, there are just 2 steps to making compost:

1. *Pile it up. Purchase a compost bin, or make one out of stiff, welded-wire fencing. Join the ends of a piece of fencing that is 4 feet high and 10 feet long. The hollow barrel you create is a perfect compost bin. Pile leaves and grass clippings in it during the year. Next spring, lift the bin off the pile, and scoop out the rich compost underneath the top layer.*
2. *Let it rot. There is no need for compost helper products. Mother Nature will make compost without your help. Experienced composters turn their piles a few times a year to make the process go faster. Organic materials will decompose whether the pile is turned or not, however. Eventually, compost will happen.*

Glossary

AAS: All-America Selections, awarded to plant varieties that have given outstanding performance in trial gardens throughout the country.

annual: a plant that starts from seed, grows, flowers, and produces a fruit and seeds in 1 season. Lettuce, corn, and beans are examples.

anthracnose: a fungus disease characterized by discolored, often dead, angular spots on leaves, stems, or fruit.

artificial potting soil: a commercial blend of peat moss, composted bark, perlite beads, or other materials used instead of soil for growing containerized plants.

banding: applying fertilizer or pesticide to the soil in a narrow strip alongside the plants as opposed to broadcasting over the entire planted area; similar to sidedressing.

bare root: plants lifted for transplanting with no soil attached to the roots.

biennial: a plant that requires 2 seasons to produce seed. It grows a rosette of foliage from seed the first year, produces a flower, fruit, and seed the second year, and dies. Examples include parsley, angelica, and carrots.

blackleg: a fungus disease characterized by black discoloration of the plant stem at and above the soil line.

black rot: a fungus disease characterized by black discoloration and rotting of the fruit, for example, of grapes or apples.

blossom end rot: a leathery brown spot that develops on the bottoms of tomatoes, or peppers or vine crops due to unfavorable growing conditions. It is usually limited to the first few fruits early in the season and is self-correcting.

bolt: to produce flowers or seed prematurely—generally referring to plants grown for their foliage such as lettuce, spinach or certain herbs.

cane: a woody, often hollow stem, usually unbranched, arising from the ground. Stems of brambles are referred to as canes.

catfacing: malformed fruit caused by poor pollination.

chlorosis: yellowing of young leaves due to failure to develop chlorophyll; often caused by high soil pH or nutrient deficiencies.

clubroot: a disease characterized by swollen, clublike roots on plants such as cabbage or broccoli.

cold hardiness: the ability of a plant to withstand the expected low temperatures in a location. Some vegetables are completely hardy and can stand winter weather; perennial vegetables and herbs such as asparagus and thyme are in this category. Some annual vegetables are semihardy and stand a freeze; peas and Brussels sprouts are examples.

come true: a characteristic of collected seed that produces a plant identical to the one from which the seed was collected. Hybrid varieties do not come true from collected seed.

companion planting: growing 2 crops in the same space or growing plants of several different varieties next to each other to reduce insect problems; for example, radishes are often sown in the same rows as carrots.

compound leaves: leaves consisting of several to many leaflets attached to a single central stem.

cross-pollination: fertilization of a flower of one variety of a plant by the pollen of another closely related plant as opposed to self-pollination.

crown: the center part of a plant; the point at which the leaves and stems of a plant join the roots.

cultivar: the correct nomenclature for a variety that is developed and persists under cultivation.

cup and receptacle: the cup-shaped fruit of raspberry or blackberry consisting of tiny cohering fruitlets covering a buttonlike receptacle. Cups of raspberries separate from the receptacle; those of blackberry do not.

determinate: growth characteristic of tomato varieties that set terminal flowers, thus stopping further growth. Determinate plants form low bushes with all of the fruit formed about the same time; they are convenient for processing.

dibble: a small, hand-held, pointed stick used to make holes in the soil for planting seedlings. Also, to poke a hole in the soil with a dibble.

dioecious: plants bearing male and female flowers on separate plants.

dormant oil: a highly refined petroleum product used as an insecticide. Dormant oils kill insects by smothering them in a film of oil.

drainage: the capacity of a soil to drain away water.

fallow: to keep soil free of all plants for a season or more, thus reducing subsequent weed problems.

fertilizer: any substance used to add plant nutrients to the soil.

foliage: leaves of plants.

frass: a mass of shredded plant parts and often insect parts due to feeding by insect pests.

frost-free date: average date of last frost (as compared to latest date of last frost).

full sun: receiving all available sunlight from sunrise to sunset.

germinate: to begin growth as a plant from a seed.

green manure: temporary planting of fast-growing vegetation to be plowed into the soil, adding organic matter and improving soil condition.

greensand: glauconite, a naturally occurring potassium-bearing mineral used as a fertilizer.

green shoulders: a condition that develops on plants such as carrots when roots are exposed to light, or tomatoes when exposed to conditions unfavorable for ripening.

growing season: the number of days between the last freeze of spring and the first freeze of autumn.

gynoecious: refers to female flowers, as in gynoecious plants, which have only female flowers.

harden off: to gradually expose plants grown indoors or in a greenhouse to lower temperatures, making it possible for them to withstand colder conditions. Also applies to plants exposed to adverse conditions such as low fertility, low temperatures, or drying, which causes stunting and sometimes premature flowering.

healing in: a method of storing plants in the ground until conditions are favorable for planting. Plants are laid on their sides in a shallow trench and covered with soil so that only the tips of the plants are exposed.

heirloom: items handed down from generation to generation. Heirloom plants or heirloom varieties have been maintained by collecting and saving seed each year. They are available from seed specialists, have not been improved and may lack the disease resistance of newer varieties, but retain the wonderful characteristics that made them popular in the past. These varieties may do very well in your garden if it is free of certain diseases.

hilling up: mounding soil around the base of a plant for various purposes, for example, to blanch celery or Belgian endive, or to protect potatoes from the sun.

hill planting: setting several plants in close proximity in a "hill," and widely spacing the "hills" in rows. (In row planting the plants are evenly spaced along the row.)

hybrid: a cultivar resulting from a cross between two dissimilar cultivars, the ensuing cultivar being different from either parent.

indeterminate: growth characteristic of tomato plants that set flower clusters along a vining stem, never setting terminal flowers. They grow indefinitely, producing fruit throughout the season until killed off by frost. These varieties are excellent for growing on trellises or stakes.

inoculant: the introduction of specific bacteria into the soil which enables legume plants to convert atmospheric nitrogen into a form suitable for plant food. Powdered inoculant is typically applied to seeds before planting.

insecticidal soap: highly refined liquid soap used as an insecticide.

insecticide: a pesticide to control insects and related pests.

latest date of last frost: the date after which frost does not occur in a locality.

leader: the central vertical shoot of a plant.

leaf spots: localized disease infections producing spots on leaves.

lifting: digging up or pulling plants, as in harvesting or removing plants for transplanting.

monoecious: plants bearing separate male flowers and female flowers on the same plant (typical of vine crops).

mosaic: a virus disease causing a mosaic pattern of discoloration in plant leaves.

mulch: a covering of straw, compost, plastic sheeting, etc., spread on the ground around plants to reduce water loss, prevent weeds, and enrich the soil.

mummy berries: tiny, misshapen, useless fruits, usually the result of disease; often refers to brambles or grapes.

open pollination: refers to plants pollinated naturally by whatever pollen happens to blow onto them. These varieties come true from seed, that is, collected seed will produce a plant identical to the one from which the seed was collected. Hybrid varieties do not come true from collected seed.

overwinter: to survive winter; to tolerate the winter conditions without injury.

partial shade: filtered sun all day or shade part of the day.

peat pot: small pot formed of peat moss.

perennial: a plant that grows from seed, developing a plant for the first year, and flowering and producing fruit and seeds each year thereafter. Rhubarb, strawberries, and apple trees are examples.

pesticide: a material used to control insects (insecticide), fungi (fungicide), or weeds (herbicide).

pH: Soil pH is a measure of acidity or alkalinity. Soil is neutral at a pH of 7.0. Above 7.0, the soil is alkaline; below 7.0, the soil is acidic. Most garden plants prefer a pH of 6.0 to 7.0.

pinch back: to remove the growing tip of a plant to stimulate branching.

pistil: the central, seed-bearing, female organ of a flower.

plug: a plant grown in a plug of soil, small pot, or plug tray.

pollination: fertilization of female part of a flower by pollen from the male part of a flower.

reseed: to seed again; often refers to plants that spontaneously drop seed, thus perpetuating themselves.

rogue: to uproot or destroy things that do not conform to a certain standard.

root cutting: a small, thin section of root used for propagation.

root division: a section of a root system used for propagation.

rosette: a circular cluster of leaves.

rototill: to till the soil using a rototiller.

row covers: sheets, blankets, or plastic covers placed over susceptible plants to prevent frost damage or insect damage; for example, miners attacking Swiss chard or cucumber beetles feeding on vine crops. Floating row covers are mats of spun-bound polypropylene that are very light, needing no supports, and do not smash plants under them.

rust: a fungus disease characterized by masses of rustlike sores on plant surfaces.

savoy: crinkled or puckered leaves, for example, savoy cabbage or savoy spinach.

scaffold: a horizontal branch on a tree.

scald: a condition in which plant leaves dry out and become papery at the edges.

seedbed: finely tilled soil suitable for sowing seed; also a bed prepared in that manner.

side-dress: to apply fertilizer next to the rows of plants at about half the normal rate, thus avoiding damage from getting fertilizer on the growing plants. Sidedressing is usually applied about midseason after the preplant fertilizers have begun to run out.

soil types: sand, silt, clay, or loam, describing the coarseness or fineness of the soil.

spur-type fruit tree: a tree that has fewer lateral branches and shortened, fruit-bearing stems called spurs. It grows more slowly, usually bears earlier, and develops into a smaller tree.

stamen: the male part of a seed-bearing flower.

suckers: undesirable shoots arising from the roots of a plant near the base or a short distance from the base.

tender perennial: a perennial plant that is unable to tolerate the winter temperatures in a particular climate.

till: to work the soil by spading, digging, cultivating, or rototilling.

tilth: physical condition of the soil.

variety: a cultivar.

vegetative propagation: propagation by means of cuttings or divisions.

water sprouts: vigorous vertical sprouts growing from the base, trunk, or scaffold branches of a tree.

whip (in relation to fruit tree): a small, single-stemmed, whiplike tree used to start a planting.

wilt: a fungus or bacterial disease that causes plants to wilt and die.

Bibliography

Bailey, L. Hyde. *Standard Cyclopedia of Horticulture.* New York: Macmillan, 1963.

Bass, Larry. *Container Vegetable Gardening.* North Carolina Cooperative Extension.

Bender, Steve. *Southern Living Garden Book.* Birmingham, Alabama: Oxmoor House, 1998.

Big Book of Gardening Skills. Pownal, VT: Garden Way Publishing, 1993.

Bradshaw, David, and Karen Russ. *Heirloom Vegetables.* Clemson University Cooperative Extension Service.

Brickell, Christopher, ed. American Horticultural Society. *The American Horticultural Society A-Z Encyclopedia of Garden Plants*, New York: Macmillan, 1989.

Chambers, Davis, and Lucinda Mays. *Vegetable Gardening.* New York: Pantheon Books, 1994.

Fernandez, Gina. *Small Fruit Cultivars for Home Use in North Carolina.* North Carolina Cooperative Extension.

Hastings, Don. *Gardening in the South with Don Hastings: Vegetables and Fruits.* Dallas: Taylor Publishing, 1987.

Johnson, Kenneth. *Landscaping with Fruit.* Tennessee Agricultural Extension Service.

Kentucky, University of. *Home Fruit Variety Recommendations: 2000,* <http://www.uky.edu/Agriculture/Horticulture/frt00recomm.pdf>

Krewer, Gerard, Thomas Crocker, Paul Bertrand, and Dan Horton. *Minor Fruits and Nuts in Georgia.* University of Georgia Cooperative Extension Service.

Lockwood, David. *Home Tree Fruit Plan.* Tennessee Agricultural Extension Service.

Lockwood, David, and Alvin Rutledge. *Tree Fruit, Tree Nut and Small Fruit Cultivar Recommendations for Tennessee.* Tennessee Agricultural Extension Service.

McLaurin, Wayne, and Sylvia McLaurin. *Herbs for Southern Gardens.* Available from the University of Georgia Agricultural Business office (phone 706-542-8999).

Musgrove, Mary Beth. *The Alabama Vegetable Gardener.* Alabama Cooperative Extension System.

Oster, Maggie. *Ortho's All About Herbs.* Des Moines: Meredith Books, 1999.

Powell, Arlie, David Himelrick, William Dozier, and Mary Beth Musgrove. *Fruit Culture in Alabama.* Alabama Cooperative Extension System.

Puls, Earl. *Suggested Fruit Varieties for Louisiana.* Louisiana Cooperative Exetension Service.

Pyzner, John. *The Louisiana Home Orchard.* Louisiana Cooperative Extension Service.

Reich, Lee. *Uncommon Fruits Worthy of Attention: A Gardener's Guide* (CD-ROM).

Relf, Diane, and Rich Marini. *Tree Fruit in the Home Garden.* Virginia Cooperative Extension.

Relf, Diane, and Jerry Williams. *Small Fruit for the Home Garden.* Virginia Cooperative Extension.

Smith, Edward. *The Vegetable Gardener's Bible.* North Adams, Massachusetts: Storey Books, 2000.

Stephens, James M. *Manual of Minor Vegetables.* Florida Extension Service Manual, 1988

Swahn, J.O. *The Lore of Spices.* New York: Crescent Books, 1997.

Swenson, Allan. *Fruit Trees for the Home Gardener.* New York: Lyon & Burford, 1994.

Thompson, H. C., and W. C. Kelly. *Vegetable Crops.* New York: McGraw-Hill, 1957.

Tiedjens, Victor. *Vegetable Encyclopedia and Gardener's Guide.* New York: New Home Library, 1943.

Warmund, Michele. *Fruit and Nut Cultivars for Home Plantings.* Department of Horticulture, University of Missouri-Columbia.

Weaver, William. *Heirloom Vegetable Gardening.* New York: Henry Holt & Co., 1997.

Plant Index

Want to know more about Tennessee gardening?

Interested in fantastic flowers for Tennessee? How about stunning Tennessee shrubs? Do you want tall, healthy Tennessee trees?

If you enjoy *50 Great Herbs, Fruits and Vegetables for Tennessee*, you will appreciate similar books featuring Tennessee flowers, shrubs, and trees. These valuable books also deserve a place in your gardening library.

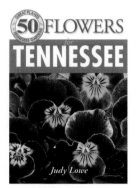

50 Great Flowers for Tennessee

Judy Lowe shares her personal recommendations on fifty delightful flowering plants for Tennessee. From colorful annuals that give you spring-to-fall color, to hard-working perennials that return year after year, you will find much to choose from in this book.

50 Great Shrubs for Tennessee

If you want guidance on great shrubs for Georgia, this is the book for you. From the boxwood to the flowering azalea, Judy Lowe shares her gardening wit and wisdom on fifty wonderful shrubs for Tennessee.

50 Great Trees for Tennessee

Author Judy Lowe recommends fifty great trees for Tennessee. She offers fantastic options on small flowering trees, great evergreens, and trees that delight with multiseason interest.

Look for each of these books today.